# Unspeakable Strangers

## Descents into the Dark Self

## Ascents into Light

UNSPEAKABLE STRANGERS, in progress for a number of years, is composed of several sequences of poems about or related to the Holocaust, its causes, and the persistence of its causes and effects. Where possible, I try to establish the relation of past, present, and future, including compromises individuals and nations make with their ideals and professed values—political, religious, and personal—in all countries and in all cultures.

The forms of the poems are varied and intentionally broken. The ironic use of haiku stanzas, in a sequence about the children; and the ironic, twisted use of the sonnet, a form traditionally celebrating fertility, try to reflect the attack on fertility and the war against life itself. These and a number of other poems here were written in response to "The Nazi Drawings" of Mauricio Lasansky. The poems are not necessarily interpretations of Lasansky's paintings, however, and the connections with the history leading to and surrounding the Holocaust are my own.

These are about half of the poems I have written related to the Holocaust. I include selected excerpts and notes from my readings—less to acknowledge sources than to attest to the basis in fact of the poems and to provide an interplay between the fact and its fictive frames. An essay, following the poems, about their history is in part a record and a response to the many questions and responses that have been made over the years as poems have been published, as I have read them to diverse audiences, or shown them to others..

# Unspeakable Strangers

## Descents into the Dark Self

## Ascents into Light

poems & an essay

by

Van K. Brock

Anhinga Press • Tallahassee, Florida • 1995

Library of Congress Cataloging in Publication Data
Brock, Van K.
*Unspeakable Strangers:*
*Descents into the Dark Self, Ascents into Light*

Library of Congress Catalog Card Number ISBN: 0938 078 42 9
Printed in the United States of America



---

Anhinga Press, Inc. is a nonprofit corporation staffed by volunteers and dedicated wholly to the publication and appreciation of fine poetry.

**COVER ART: from Mauricio Lasansky's *The Nazi Drawings, Copyright 1966*, by Mauricio Lasansky Foundation. Permission of the Lasansky Corporation, Iowa City, IA. Owned by The Levitt Foundation, Minneapolis, Minnesota.**

This publication is sponsored in part by a grant from the Florida Department of State, Division of Cultural Affairs, and the Florida Arts Council.

# contents

## The Ground



## Photos from the Eastern Front



## Fathers and Brothers



## Witnesses

## The Dance of the Apes



## In the Aftermath

# The Ground

*The interpretation of all images is a philosophical problem.*
E.H. Gombrich, *Art and Illusion*

*A bad work of art is the unsuccessful attempt to become conscious of a given emotion: it is what Spinoza calls an inadequate idea of an affection. Now a consciousness which thus fails to grasp its own emotion is a corrupt or untruthful consciousness.*
R.G. Collingwood, *The Principles of Art*, Oxford, 1938, 282.

*I saw a mass of matter of a dull and gloomy color between the North and East, and was informed that this mass was human beings, in as great misery as they could be, and live; and that I was mixed up with them and henceforth I must not consider myself a distinct or separate being.*

*The Journal of John Woolman*

*The poem is like a monster against which the critic does battle. There is only one way to conquer the monster: you must eat it, bones, blood, skin, pelt, and gristle. And even then the monster is not dead, for it lives in you, is assimilated into you, and you are different and somewhat monstrous yourself for having eaten it.*

Robert Penn Warren

# The Hindenberg

This early showpiece of the Thousand Year Reich
used 850,000 skins of cattle for hydrogen bags.

It is said that the night it burned
the thunder of panicking hooves
drowned the screams of passengers.

As far away as the buttes of Asia,
one old Siberian woman says that merely
the echo of their lowing still stirs
immense winds and whirlwinds.
All the small
meadows of Europe remember their grazing;
cattle-cars and railway platforms shudder
still at their foreshadowings.
Untold cobblers
recall the million seams glued and stitched
on screaming machines before their pockets
held enough hydrogen to kindle a conflagration.

The war on nature begun,
eventually, every country in Europe
and many in Africa and Asia were gutted:
in bombings, in battle, at sea, and in the fires,
filth, and hunger of virulent slave pens:
the outward rendering of ageless accumulations
sucked up from the cities and villages of earth,
and the ruins run in and out of us all,
stretching before and behind
for far more than a Thousand Years.

# For *The Nazi Drawings* of Mauricio Lasansky

Each warped character, roughly mirroring
us, sees through his living space only
part of a face he skillfully distorts
or can't bear. We pass through these eyes
into history uncoiling backwards from
the climacteric of a rhythmically punctuated
orgasm, a violent encephalogram threatening
us, still. These are not malevolent
inventions. They help us not to forget
this sorrow, to the living, is necessary
baptism and catechism, confirming
that to survive these victims means we must
be sired by and born of ravaged fathers
and mothers or be left in the begetting dark.
We cannot turn away from their rending
images of ourselves. Their suffering still
cries out—to be grasped, to be grieved.

# They Asked Him Why

The condor chained to the thief of fire
he devours never asks why sparrows tuft
their nests with down from their throats,
or why his is littered with cells of flesh.
Sockets where he dipped his whittled beak
hold abatoirs deep with the ink of sunsets.
My daughters cover their eyes when I open
my sky-blue spheres. Stars. My wife shudders.
They beg for the merciful wax Odysseus gave
his mariners as the sea absorbed red tides:
You curse us with winter vistas. Your fingers
torn off like twigs bleed sap all spring
reminding us of the green cedars of Lebanon.

Forests strive through him. Ax-shouldering men
mount the people smiling snowthroated lullabies
to balm their blue ears. Horned, they sow again,
erupt with evangelists, teachers, cankers.
He breaks into quaking aspen, lindens, ash.
Eyeless Mums and Glads empty each child's sockets
to plant the bulbs of sacred searing ways.
The one-eyed rule from knots far back of their noses,
without depth of field, gutting what they mimic,
maiming the toddler they say leads them, her good eye
twitching. A west wind howls out of Carcassone,
where Romans camped, up a muddy stream, and moans
through scraggly fields until it finds the river
where a dry fountain of song crumbles near the banks
of the ravaged city of light. He falls weeping.
Tongues of ash turning into green flames lick
his eyes and mouth with the book of syllables.

## The One Moon

*Liberation is not achieved except by perceiving the identity of individual spirit with universal spirit . . . . Disease not cured by saying the name of the medicine, but by taking the medicine.*
**Shankara**

Though in our night we seldom see the sun,
the moon empties itself, bearing light.
Every sheet of water reflects the moon,

But if we come between moon and sun
spiders dance on crackled webs,
eclipse, drybeds, flat notes.

Those who look for light in absences
of others, stumble in turbulence.
They cannot hear the symphony.

Lakes shimmer, the moons waver, exposed plates
of holograms break, again and again,
and each part still holds all spheres entire,

each smaller piece more faintly.
Then scattered sharps forget the silent chorus,
music shatters in slivers,

but the orchestra in its spacious auditorium
knows only boundaries we imagine or endure.
I would eat these pilferings and be cured.

# PHOTOS FROM THE EASTERN FRONT

*In days like these, it seems as though people are victims of an epidemic and not responsible for their actions. The germs of this special epidemic undermine the constitution of the person and change it. People act as though in fever. How can one blame a patient in delirium? Fear of the Revolution has altered their souls, or rather dug out the subconscious qualities which were dormant, thus upsetting the patient's ethical balance, and the values he had believed in in the past. He is capable of actions and neglects which he never would have committed in a normal state. One should therefore not judge people from the state they are in now. In normal conditions they would have kept to the rules and moral standards they had been brought up in, and, if this great upheaval had not taken place, they would have remained decent gentlemen. I want to believe that, at the time I knew and loved them, they were their real selves.*

*The Memoirs of Catherine Karolyi*
George Allen & Unwin, Ltd., 1966 (p. 210)

*The people who had awakened for a short time have again been put to sleep with the help of narcotic catchwords. The masses have again been betrayed.*

*'The policy of the international had to be subordinated to ...Russian policy.... Whole sets of the best functionaries in Europe [were] physically liquidated. They crushed their own organizations abroad and co-operated with ... reactionary countries ... to suppress the revolutionary meetings which came at the wrong moment. They betrayed their friends and compromised with their enemies. Their press and ...schools cultivate chauvinism, militarism, dogmatism, conformism and ignorance. The arbitrary power of the government is ... unexampled in history.'*

*'The energies of this generation are exhausted ... in the revolution. For this generation is bled white and there is nothing left of it but a moaning, numbed, apathetic lump of sacrificial flesh.' 'I see the flayed body of the generation, but I see no trace of the new skin.' That's how Rubasoff sees it now, but for ten years he had talked the same language as Glatkin, the son of that revolution which Rubasoff had brought to victory and which is now holding him in a steel grip.*

*We would like to throw it off as 'purely Russian,' the twisted pathological problems of diseased brains. But Koestler's book is much more than Russian or Communist. It is the eternal conflict of thesis and antithesis..... What has to come first; the change of the individual who will then adopt the better institutions to his better and higher ideals, or the change of the institutions so that the individual who could not change otherwise should develop? For how can we change man, if the conditions under which he lives, have made him what he is? Can one build up a new world with old people? Can one hope to breed new people in a rotten world? [The] means ... are such that no man using them can escape from deterioration in human value. Can one build anything worthwhile on such a humanity? ....From all times people have used bad means to obtain good ends, or rather ends they thought good. [We] accept mass murder and violence to resist a much greater evil—the permanent violence of fascism. The principle of preventive wars. Wars to make the world safe for democracy.... The balance is overthrown, the brakes give, and mankind runs amuck towards destruction. [We] cannot turn vice into virtue without having the vital centres from which human evolution grows damaged. Moral balance is essential to preserve us from disintegration. As long as we preserve in them the faith of absolute good, faith in love, truth and justice, there is still hope for progress. Oversimplification does not ... mean clearsightedness, and the allegation that there is no difference between the methods of democracies and those of totalitarian states, can mislead only the simple-minded who disregard the importance of measure and degree and are ignorant of the art of differentiation. To follow a thought to its last conclusion can be a pleasure, but it is not life. Life is complex and paradoxical; its pattern is composed by varying hues, lights and shades, and no rigid dogma deviates from its rhythm of ebb and flow from the harmony of its inner law.*

Catherine Andrassy [*Karolyi*], "The Theory of Justice,"
HORIZON IV/19 (July 1941)—on Arthur Koestler's *DARKNESS AT NOON*).

# The Mirror

Back of the light, mercurial darkness.
Nothing.  Mirror a trick door. Dawn.
In and out. Skull thickens.
The buttoned collar snugs his neck.

His fires purge the gene pool: history,
nation, race. They once thought him
only a dunce.  Now they see
how the folk soul bears him.
                                        Helga,
his woman,
                  Volkheart of the Year,
writes stories of the age in praise
of the reichsglories
                              for the kinderblitz:

how one must live in the moment, but die
to bring our dream of the past to the future,
how actresses, the rich, the obsequious,
crossed channels and oceans and came
to the spell he wove with a bitter-honey tongue
over the minions of his cross of scythes,
whose standards for our women and youth,
etc., frankly, we cannot gloss,
how books, read correctly, call us forth.

Surf rages in their night.

Wodan's ravens—Thought, Memory—spur his eyes;
the wolves—Ravener and Greed—tear her nostrils:
ammonia  fabulizes goats whose smoke blots out sun;
curved-horn rams graze her scarlet dawns:

Lost innocence shrivels his mouth.
Stench escapes from her lips.

# Engineer

Helmet a skull cocked slightly, he looks
through empty goggles. His lower lip frees
itself; a collar climbs his chin to defy
what dulls his eyes, his exposed white tunic.

Machine guns, tattling all night of mass
burials, bother him. These seeds will grow.
The doctors and their experiments unnerve him.
His own probings look brutal, but what's done,
he writes his wife, splinters soldiers
seasoned through humiliation. They become inhuman.
He will pave and epitomize modernity with raw will.

The Becker moving van asphyxiates the living
enroute to the ditch, efficiently recycling
fumes into such contortions his men must work
on vodka to force the death angels to remove
the mired bodies. And his showers of mist
like fire will civilize this smoke-vomiting maw,
whose fuel, still alive in huts of excrement—
herded, stunned by maggots and lice—hurtle,
night and day. Elegant lasers enter his dreams
where entire populations vanish without a trace.

Back home, they purify even the language, seldom
murmuring, knowing, pretending not to. Poof!
to pastors or priests who protest. Their clothes
are no whiter than his. Today or yesterday:
he does not change, as they do. Otherwise,
sealed in deaf Beethoven, he learns from Faust
how perfect love cancels the pact with evil.

On his tunic a black, seven-fingered handprint,
an invisible, immaculate shadow he cannot see:
a flight of ravens    a menorah    a cry of ash.

# Efficiency Award

The bridgework visor over his eyes shows
how weary he grows of these walking sties.

He strokes his luger     mists it blue
with his breath
                    polishes     cocks it
bites the barrel
                    laughs.

They'll stand all night in snow;
no water, no relief: a natural selection.
Who raises an eye discovers a new world.

His ear can't elude shrieks that stitch sleep
and bind his days. Will he, they, their next
of kin, if any survive, believe this place
more than a nightmare? Against the will
of his lip, he sinks into his tunic.
It enters his mouth: a bridle.

                                        Grandchildren
of his grandchildren's grandchildren will wake
with his nightmares, but he has begun the book
of the future:

Truth is whatever you write on paper
people will subscribe to or buy.

He strains to learn to be both god and beast,
rider and ridden. Lashed to his heels, spurs
bite his flanks. Two bits grind his teeth.

# *Die Briefe* (The Letters)

*Cherie,*

When this was taken
I was with a ski brigade looking westward
from an eastern mountain, toward you.
The white uniform is for camouflage.
Despite the desolate spaces here,
it's difficult to get an uncluttered photograph.
The circular object to my right is not
a baby's skull. It's the sun.
The thread stuck through my lip
is knotted to hold a needle.
Here I must do my own mending.

*Meine Lieber Frau,*

A snapshot for you and the children.
You see how my affection turns.
I am a medical technician assigned to a factory
with many comforts and plenty of clean uniforms.
The new snow on the ground is very pure.
The skull on my right is not an ostrich egg;
it's a ball covered with the membranes of irises.
Such curiosities here are ordinary.

The children will learn to see themselves
in my photograph.

There's no shadow in my eyes,
nor hole in my forehead.
I've stitched myself to the state.
Often the air fills with dark smoke.

*Mein Mutterchen,*

A photo for you and Papa.
Some of us boys were playing kickball.
You see the kickball to my left.
(It's to my right; this negative is reversed.)
You'll like to know I have charge of thousands,
my own stapler and paperclips,
a desk set with a pen like a rapier. God!
The stench!

The thread's hanging from my mouth
because I couldn't remove the needle.
There's no falcon over my eyes.
A flashlight of darkness
shines from a hole in my forehead.

# The New Man

A twisted cross grows a black rose
through a sleeve, from an arm. Medals clot
his tunic. A raw sun rises in a cracked mirror
as he twists a fist behind him and squeezes.
Not even awake, he snaps gartered heels, Heils!
his mirror,
                    "To the world purified,"
          drops
                    the erected arm.
Petrified, his old roommate
echoes, purifications castrate civilizations.

He may never stay quiet in his head,
but he won't ask anyone again, Where would Rome
or Greece, whose grandeurs you covet, be
without their pantheons of tribes?," then add,
A racist, with no help, will rape himself.

He sees himself in Afghanistan, Chile, the shady
clean Veldt, in rice paddies proving himself,
again, surrounded now by sweltering umber slaves,
his people always behind him, always hungering,
More room! The World!

He pulls flowers from his own heart to twist
into a bouquet of old perennials—
Rancor, Ignorance, Envy, Arrogance—
their seeds will flower for a Thousand Years.

He starts his new day with vodka,
the whitened blood of Poland, a new man.

# The Web

*the lesion from which man suffers is within*
Trigant Burrow

Many spiders. One web. Left. Right.
Scattered points. Broken diagonals.
Each vying leg, trying to tread the center,
lost in itself, stirred chaos, and neutrals
paralyzed, one said, "I will create order,"
then his brown armies webbed and ate
this small band, then that.

His black mass,
immune to light, squatted dead center,
defecating luminous decay.
It danced around him, devouring, devoured.
Few resisted. Many fled. Others,
revelling in wavy mirrors, fur
of another—stolen nuance, torn idea—
dreamt themselves larger, lovelier.
Night strutted day, encircling
the stunned, the stilled, as hordes
watched or joined aberrant hunger.
Web fused to web.
While on peaceful white threads,
celibate white-throated Parthenogenisites
moved ritually, prayerfully, in flowing
red gowns, or black, white, brown,

as brown soldiers, blackening into mutants,
waddled and ruled all webs,
the white occult center darkening.

# WARPED ZERO

Sticky music spools fused shapes webbing
all in its death-in-life aria, only language,
pus of skewed hungers.

Anyone unusual feeds his appetites:
whoever refuses, whoever he chooses.
His spewing tongues gnash their paracletes,
suborning many accomplices, then killing them.
Few who survive refuse to serve him.

Dried legs join dessicate bodies
of old cunning—skeletal tyrannies
wanting their flesh back—with banal, good
citizens, who, shocked, they insist,
sadly, want to get on.
                                        Many falter.
We spin many denials.
                                        Few escape knowing.
Cracked mudflats, folds,
                                        creases of maps
running off edges, seas meeting under earth,
returning, in bloody gulfs, binding—
threads broken between stars.

Lines of longitude and latitude
charting, measuring the globe
pulled out of sphere by our swervings.

Cracks in being. Our contrarieties.

# Mutant Aesthetics

*The crime that is latent in us, we must*
*inflict on ourselves . . . not on others..*
J. M. Coetzee

Blurred lines, scrossed staffs, everyday
    metronome bureaucracies: gullies, furnaces.
Excited by sentiment and prurience, spiritual
    and physical mutilation, he draws his tempo
from individuals and nations, to orchestrate
    the bent ecstasies and shrieks of obedients
with wrenching incomprehension—selves dissolved
    in rallies to swell his chorus,
his solace.
            Echoing our dank proclivities,
he howls and coos the twisted knowings
    of the maimed into a bootcamp chorus,
he weaves a burning tapestry—black, red, white—
    with deadly incestuous purity.

*Lentamente, fortissimo, crescendo*
He wraps them in unspeakable conversions,
makes a flag of a cross, all arms broken,
pitched in a livid ring on a ground of blood,
as others stand by, secure, in silence.
Them: *the flayed body of a generation,*
*but no trace of a new skin, no new man,*
*only a moaning numb lump of raw flesh.*

## How Mutants Are Made

The loss of one sense alters all others.
The right brain severed from the left,
the left hand wrestles with the right,
but one lobe anesthetized, no opposition.
The long blind, regaining sight, see blobs
of clashing color, and sometimes, in hysteria,
balance skewed, revert to blindness before
shocked senses resynthesize order—
any unity preferred to total confusion.
Terror reorients. People, like children,
emulate authority when punishments are sudden,
irrevocable, rewards venial or vital. Cultures
evolved over centuries crumble in days.

Half-wakened in half-worlds split within,
lulled back to sleep by narcotic catchtones
simplifications, sensuous music—then faced
with surrender or death, they reflect
the conductor's erratic torrent
as he looks in them to dimly find himself
in stagnancy he drinks from.

Reborn in his zero consciousness,
they are already dead.

He draws his dreams from their wells, he says,
and the more outrageous his claims,
more terribly his dreams become
their nightmare: simpler speech,
hollower values, rawer symbols, scapegoats
to die for their sins, to let them believe
in their innocence again.
In tightening, widening covens
they betray themselves and each other,
becoming agents, murderers.

# The Fly

A one-winged fly buzzes loudly as it sputters
in a closed spiral, up, down, its energy spent
in redundancies. The expedient adjust always:
exploiters, the exploited. Cruelty breeds
crude converts: stick figures, jacksteps, barks.

"The banality of evil's hard to believe,"

said Heidegger, a subtle man
who sank into drivel and replaced
the rector who defied Goebbels,
"and boring."
Some serve, as many claim, to keep madmen out;
others think they spawn new values.

Atrocities spool from hairline cracks of dryrot.
Most, given a chance, obeyed rules or kept quiet.

Women who would not bear sons,
devious fathers who did not wing them,
pintsized professors who did not buzz
in downward mayfly spirals, and all among us
who save themselves and their families
saving neighbors and strangers, sharpening
silences underground, learning sabotage
to stay sane and human amidst madness.
Those few count more than the many imagine.

## The Elite of the Elite

New houses hollowed from old rock.
We drive new pikes through Europe.
Vienna opens her knees.
London, Moscow, Paris, the Americas—
all look away as we crack Prague,
Belgium, the Ukraine—fleas, as eager
as we in our procedures.
                                        Ho hum.
What small country do we ravage today.

'Monstrous,' the timorous say,
as we sweep up all oddities,
all otherness. Garbage!

            The degradations they bear!

If some give sanctuary to refugees
starving their Nazi in the cellar—
we free them!
                              You who think I'm dead—
buried under your cellar stairs—
dig me up. Dare.
                                If he discovers cavities,
he hides them, blurring complexities,
assuring his victims, amusedly,

*Who will believe you lived or died—or care?*

# The Leader of the People

He carried a whip with a loaded handle,

longed for the Tower of London
where Henry beheaded his wives.

Was an artist, made vulgar drawings
of a niece, his forced mistress,
ordered her suicide, humiliated
compliant Eva, others.

Loved families and children.
Cronies slipped him snapshots and movies
where parent and child, brother and sister,
had to watch each other—starved, brutalized.

They knew his tastes. They paid dearly.

His wardens forced a modest, starved family,
both parents and children, naked, to sing
sugartit lieder for the leader.

He loved live music. And movies.

Every night a movie—in one of his favorites,
a superhuman ape
(triumphant mechanics and trick photography)
saves the typed blonde and savages her city
in his raging consummation.

And the people—the people hailed him.

# Pragmatic Undersoul

Smart devil. His uncluttered views fuse.
Sure, he's crude but his music stirs people;
he dreams a continent his autobahns web.
I thought we weren't ready yet. My wife
and I like Goethe, Bach, even Brecht
poking our shams, but, look, populations
double; overmen are only sneaky burghers
really—you know, more jobs, lower taxes,
all make killings. It all trickles down.
We simply know how to think clearly. Look,
whoever succeeds where others fail become
easier targets than those who the bolsheviks bait.
Know a good thing. Blend.
Only the chosen care who's chosen.
Ah! We resent that, too—Jesus!
Churches rot souls the way swamp air rots
good fir boats: we vacate on altars,
dump on God, grow no inner base.
Perfect obedience redeems those he chooses.
Forget that Nordic Christ crap Rosenberg rants
and Goebbels peddles. Let it divert Lutherans
or Catholics who want diversion.
The Fuehrer's still Catholic.
Pius sleeps with us.

## Fathers and Brothers

*. . . form is disclosed to the artist as he looks at what is over against him. He banishes it to be a 'structure'. This 'structure' is not in a world of gods, but in this . . . world of men. It is certainly 'there', even if no human eye seeks it out . . . .*

Martin Buber

Wodan means "one who makes mad." He is god of inspiration and illusion, an arch-deceiver, Lord of the Kingdom of Death and ancestor of German kings. His wolves were Ravener and Greed; his ravens Thought and Memory.

information from *The Book of Norse Mythology*

*Man is summoned to . . . really live in a godless world, without attempting to gloss over or explain its ungodliness in some religious way or other . . . .   When we speak of God in a "non-religious" way, we must speak of him in such a way that the godlessness of the world is not in some way concealed but for that reason revealed rather in, and thus exposed to, an unexpected light.*

Dietrich Bonhoeffer

# This Way to the Gas

For Tadeusz Borowski (1922-1951)

Tadeusz, the vice is still tight, and you
among those who show how it works—jaws, screw,
and lever—through what we do or don't do.
With you gone, we all still write your life
and are written on, as it outlines us, still.
So many players, such footwork, kicked spheres,
the game in overtime, and Poland back and forth
for 200 years, between new-risen czars mocking
Christ and Rome. And after our Armistice, Poland
fought on in rubble, then during the brief breath
of the Republic of '22, you were born, a Pole
in the Ukraine, without a voice. Europe's lights
flickering after another long nightmare—reservoirs
of your spirit in libraries and museums elsewhere—
and bereft of tools, livestock, crops, Poland
stood up in debates and polls. Fields bloomed,
but the struggle against dead souls who still want
to live through us, goes on. I hear you, Tadeusz.

Your dad in the Polish army fought old gauntlets
making the gamerules around you. You were four
when he was gulagged to dig canals from Leningrad
through tundra, to the White Sea, but already eight
when your mother, sent to Siberia, nearly died
among thousands who starved. You studied, tended
the cows until their calves calved, and you were 10.
Your dad came home, a stranger; mine died, and I
was born where white still taunted black; all that
in the year that became Hitler, Hitler a nation,
deepening poverty everywhere, darkening earth still.

Your mother returned; you were 12, the years lost;
and all together in Warsaw, poverty sent you off
to school with the Brothers of Poverty, almost
as much an orphan as Poland. The blitz hit you
at 17, and east and west left you to SS squads
rounding up Poles for medals. In a close race,
a single squad shot 140,000 the first 24 hours.

All schools closed to Poles, in Warsaw's rooms
teachers rose tall to tell you the true heritage
of Europe, your struggle and trampling. On the way
to your finals, cars blocked streetcars, like tigers
tracking antelope, you said, as you spilled from wild
trolleys, ripe green pears, tearing up tilled fields,
spring scents. In jungle streets people were hunted.

It was 1940. At 18, in the underground university,
you read literature, translated *Twelfth Night*"—If music
be the food of love, play on, Give me excess of it...—
fell in love,—"Methought she purged the air of pestilence.
. . . fell and cruel hounds E'er since pursue me"—
and printed your own poems, among banned bulletins,
for us: "We will leave scrapiron behind us,
in hollow mocking mouths of laughing generations."

In the rooms of a friend they tortured, the SS trapped
your fiancee, then you. From your cell by the ghetto,
you saw soldiers lobbing grenades into huge tenements,
burning houses edging anguish and hunger.

You, too, went to Auschwitz, she to Birkenau,
but gassing of Aryans had stopped. The long lines
to diurnal-nocturnal flames were reserved for Jews
and the living dead you called "muslims," the bigotry
of those dying in the teeth of bigotry. Dissident
Poles and others—from the nations of Europe—waited
their turn, with able, skilled Jews, working at death

to be free. They sent you to Birkenau with a crew
to collect the day's corpses of infants, and you saw
your betrothed, her head shaved, body a raw field
of drying sores, and holding her, you said,
"Don't worry. Our children won't be bald."

As the Allies neared, you were sent to Dachau,
then American camps, among ten million homeless.
Since she was safe in Sweden, you walked away
from all slants, to wander with books and notebook
by lakes, found Paris a lovely city, giddy whore,
and returned to Warsaw to publish your whole truth,
for the American 7th Army which freed us from hell.

Your truth was brutal, even to yourself, but others,
with you in the camps, called you a friend and hero.
At 24—one of the best writer's in the east, risen
from death, deathless—your longing letters joined
you with your long betrothed. Enough! No more!
Nothing can ever be as before.
                                        Eventually,
you joined the Party, wrote its angles, stepping
on your poems, you said, as the SS had cracked
the necks of the beaten. Again, a player in history,
as our players say, and after those exams,
they sent you to a city of checkpoints, the wall still
only in the mind, but your pen a screw for old jaws
Moscow-Berlin—still chewing you, and you passed
returned, calling America the abyss, Polish Security
now torturing the friend the SS once cracked to trap
your love, then you—as those we arm do, in Haiti,
Guatemala, Chile. Tadeusz, we are disappointed lovers
blood runs from our deafened ears and muted mouths.
I, too, love her even as the wanton abuse her. Like you,
I'll not sing the end with the killers of the dream
who tell us, *The People's Justice is Never Wrong,*
and offer sweet Party tarts to taste, Paris, Warsaw,
wherever.
                    After your daughter's birth, you left
your wife in the hospital holding your bald innocence.
At home, not yet 30, tattooed still, you opened the gas.
No one's laughing, Tadeusz. *The dead are never right,*
you once wrote, *the living never wrong.* Wrong.

## For My Countrymen

After Nietzsche's *Ecce Homo*, 1888

By overmen I meant freer, higher spirits: human—
half saint, half genius—but our scholarly oxen
accuse me of dog-eat-dog, or sick hero worship.
Should I voice my dread? Faced with huge choice,
my compatriots will again strain to birth me
a mouse or a rat. Their folk soul sires
only dubious thinkers, unconscious copycats,
and the gothic soul will botch the honor
of embracing the first honest spirit in history.
They exhale dirty air I cannot breathe near,
whited sepulchres betraying themselves in words
and mien. This reflex, trying to face themselves,
they call deep. They dare not stand in light.
Tapeworms eat their hearts. They rot in summer
but cling to the limb, nauseously sweet. Terror
tells me one will insult me as a saint and play
the devil with me. Saints! How dishonest.

I unfold the next two centuries: what comes is set.
All Europe has moved, decades now, in tortured
tension, a wild river clawing earth in its course,
violent swampfart—religious, regional malaise—
afraid to reflect or know rage impels to disaster.
Our values to now root a noose of nihilisms
a moral view of life fouling with lies
the hightuned sense of truth the pious abuse.
Had Jesus lived longer, he would have loved life
and earth more and been holier. From ropemakers,
dragging out string to twist while walking backwards,
deliver us. I ask of the honey of your soul
that your dying not blaspheme man nor earth.
Of what is great, be silent or speak unequivocably.

# Hang It All, Ezra Pound

The Hero as Biography of the Age

Where did your road become swamp, old croc?
The lizard between my window and screen
shrinks daily in his straits.
Two Ezras help me see our seismic fault:
our common glass backed with quicksilver,
a rose of light pierces the trick mirror,
and we see through to you, naked,
*mon frere, posseur*, pedant, Miniver.

What a cramped space he wobbles in!
Confucious shrunken to Muss, Rapallo's bay
traded for Pisa's stripped quarries. Fine tunes
plucked from the air and laced with obscenities.

He suns on my mullion, legs violet stems
on an asparagus tip, a stolen hasid's beard
his tail. Thou knowest not head from tail.
Wild sparks of obsequious rhetoric breed
the dark with obscene growths, as plagues
incubate germs. Who weeds the garden?
Does the victor dream the green world,
or who are they who keep their souls entire?

A doomsday survival machine, locked in his own
eye, skitters on my pane, our pound of light
laced with *ignis fatuus*. Ez, where
*were* the pure villains you ranted
when you raved war? If the lidless eye cracks
in Pisa's lit night, I didn't trap my lizard
and can't free you. And philosophers play
with their expediencies, and in stupor,
we fail to cry the murderers' names,
though the sane cry their own
in dreams, or in streets, like the mad.

# The Behaviorist

When they arrest you, you say, why me,
I've not done anything—
why my parents, my wife, my children.

They take you in trucks to trains.
After three days in cattlecars,
without water, and nauseous
from feces you've not yet learned
to recycle undigested parts of,
ingrained proprieties come to you
like Job's friends, saying,
"Had you not sinned, this could not be."
"God is just; this must be punishment."
The old syllogisms.

You perceive that those around you
must also be guilty, their suffering just:
when they put children in separate cars,
double deckers (for reeducation camps,
they said), you realize they will die
in transit, or on arrival.

One cooperates, accepts injustice as
necessary to greater justice, confesses,
begs forgiveness, proves oneself—loyal,
worthier than those who will eat rats
before they acknowledge the rights
of raw power, despise those who do not see
your options, believe you had options.

You report the misconduct of fellow prisoners
and rise to the top like cream in a fetid room
absorbing the odors of the room.
The more you ingratiate yourself,
the more contempt you show those who won't learn.
You are a superior being.

# The Hunger

The face darkens, withdraws,
swallowed by a swollen skull
in its last long act of hunger.

He wears this helmet to carry bones,
a little earth-oven hat.
He turns dark inside it
and almost disappears
in boots and baggy coveralls.

These piggyback bones' skeletal fingers
cup his clasped hand,
their head fallen on his shoulder.

These bones know him.
a neighbor or a relative, perhaps.
They hold his waist in their jaws.
The feet had been frostbitten.

First his spirit was killed
by hunger and hard labor
then his body died.

His hunger could consume his killers
forever. Devour, gnaw, chew, grind,
but never digest them.

*When the last layers of subcutaneous fat had vanished, and we looked like skeletons disquised with skins and rags, we could watch our bodies beginning to devour themselves. The organism digested its own protein, and the muscles disappeared.*

Viktor Frankl, *Man's Search for Meaning*

*When we open our eyes under water we recognize objects, shapes, and colors although through an unfamiliar medium . . . . Every time we meet with an unfamiliar . . . transposition, there is a brief moment of shock and a period of adjustment—but it is an adjustment for which the mechanism exists in us.*

*[The wax image] often causes us uneasiness because it oversteps the boundary of symbolism.*

E.H. Gombrich

# Witnesses

*. . . step by step we had to become accustomed to a terrible and immense horror.*

*The prisoner who had lost faith in the future—his future—was doomed.*

Viktor Frankl

*[In] July 1943, Msgr. Angelo Giuseppe Roncalli [later Pope John Paul XXIII] wrote to Msgr. Giovanni Battista [later Pope Paul VI], a close aide of Pius XII. . . . Roncalli remarks* almost casually *that he had* chided* *[a German diplomat in Ankara] over 'the millions of Jews sent to Poland and annihilated there.'*

*Newsweek* (4/16/1973, p. 69) *Emphasis added here.

# The Witness

*(for Terrence Des Pres)*

Boxcars so packed only half could sit and breathe;
heels, hats, crisp suits, cologned, jammed in
with rags, suitcases of battered heirlooms,

or such small comforts as ease relocation;
no rest stops, toilets, nor space for privacy;
humid bodies fetid, waste caking clothes to skin;

nor rest ever for the asthmatic wheezes scraping
across the labored puffing of the train; tongues,
like charcoal, unable to block sobs or babbles

as numbing cracks to reveal jabs like ice-picks,
and nothing halts when the train jolts stopped
to feed the hissing valves and the high whines

of the whistle with coal and water. Hungers
born then cry more insistently than the shrill
steel wheels of the new cars switching in.

After three breaking days, brief overture to a long
cacophonous dirge, in the stale hold of their Middle Passage,
some died from small jolts while others meshed with pain:

her infant unable to sleep, her nipples bled strange
comforts to hold the mind in focus. Who could hope
to wake in bed, or to imagine a new world like

this: doors violently opened; stenched air swapped
for acrid smoke in a mist of ash; chimneys spitting
eerie light night and day into a sky no one ever saw

a bird fly through; glinting SS barking exits; snarling
K-9s shaking children and old men; sluggish streams,
dammed, driven apart, families rent; heirloom rings

and watches, every ornament and garment stripped;
privacies sacked, shorn thousands funnelled into frayed
uniforms, the shoes of the unnumbered, tattoos.

All changed, some woke, some never rose from the dark
hold into a new world the world refused to believe.
Hunger, exhaustion, continual humiliation, endemic

dysentery; no control; and twelve hours work, no food,
no latrines. Later, you waited—tried to—to squat
over ditches where you died if a board broke or you fell.

You used and saved a stinking rag, torn from a still-worn
cuff or hem, and you kept some watery soup to bathe with
or lost sanity, your soul, perhaps, to filth.

Stench of the living mingled with the too sweet stench
of the fires. Always, we survived to resist, record,
witness. Sleep, deep sleep, was death, and on those
edges nightmare relieved the reality it meshed with.

You woke soon or died before scabs formed new selves.
Most died—if not gassed at once—in those first days,
before they woke from dream or brain ferreted pattern

from the wild river, before they found a way to escape
the lists, to be of use. Self splits into observer
and sufferer, the knower of unknowing. Not to know

is death. The wakened, alert always, resisted always,
pushing against it, from above, below, all sides—
as swimmers push in water where all is stasis—all

structured death. We could live three months on food
they allowed, if we didn't die for lack of shoes,
clothes, medicine: to disobey or to obey was death.

Outlaws of spirit, in contradiction's jaws, we built
networks of salvage in sties of death and served death
to curb it, to save ourselves and any others we could.

Those drowning have little pity to spare the drowning.
It wasn't pretty, this do as you would be done by.
When an inmate propped me off the frozen ground,

I knew I had to stand to cheat them of my death.
Out of levees of bodies and rivers of the living
dead, laws grew quick as thistles. To steal bread

from another was murder. Fragile cords we hung by
showed few threads of compassion, but the sick
who persevered might receive bread we had saved

against our own starvation. Such threads held us.
We covered for others when possible or stopped those
whose daring or dread would bring blood on us all.

Don't define us, if you weren't there. Off daily trains,
the entranced drifted into furnaces or strayed into
bullets through acts shaped in worlds prior to that

we woke to. Though we did our best to save them, they,
like saints or heroes from other worlds, made the quotas
for us. In truth, few if any survived without freely
giving and receiving goods and favors in those sties.

# The Faucets

. . . one or two per second died
just at Auschwitz. Not
a kitchen faucet's steady drip, but all faucets,
house and yard, suburbs and cities of Europe,
dripping at once:

Sachenhausen Oranienburg Dachau
Lvov Janowska,
Over 150 camps Warsaw,
in Poland alone Treblinka,
Vilma,
not counting ghettos Ponar,
starved burned machine-gunned
Kiev
buried alive in cavernous trenches Babi Yar,
people funnelled
Lublin, Buchenwald,

worked starved Belsec,
Sobibor, Riga,
shipped in lots Lodz,
Minsk Chelmno,
from Berlin, Amsterdam, Maidanek,
Belsen,
Bergen,
Prague, Paris, Vienna, Ravensbruck,
Auschwitz,
Budapest, Belgrade Birkenau,

Bucharest, Athens

the capitals and ghettos of Europe to Auschwitz,
Wouldn't the Pope have broken with his plumber . . .
for such a loss? . .
Killed one or two per second just at Auschwitz.
And less than one per minute on the whole Western Front.

Where's a metaphor not too violent, mild?
All built in. Humiliation engineered with more
precision than any efficient use. Every way
they entered us. Guns, bullets, gas,
extensive deprivations. They savaged the soul
with inhuman organization. Their passion
was for dominance—cool paranoid murder
fixed dead center on ill-chosen targets
yearning to hold lives in we say hands
like yours or mine, look, palms delicate
and cross-veined as the Pope's
who never held living tissue of his own, who
knowing all, never lifted a pen in protest—
featherless birds, to hold at will,
knowing you know if he lets you live
his whim can have your body, life,
day or night. One or two a second, day
and night, clockwork, just at Auschwitz.
Man, woman, child, doll—commodities:
usable, disposable. They wanted needed
our indispensable dignities mass nudity,
bodies wasting in rags. In immaculate
uniforms, they mired us in our excrement.

Who finds such fetishes erotic? How?
They did not want merely our deaths.
The dead flew through us like shrill
silent bats from a burning barn.
In this confessional, delicate, practiced
hands extracted every secret, gold
and silver of the mouth, jewels of womb
and intestine, oils from our bodies—
but what did they want?

# Earth Goddess

She married a Jew,
but since she was a Christian,
they shipped both off,
keeping her for their whore.

Widowed on her nuptial night.

This shattered glass
is a blank slate, they thought.

But from her shards, a mosaic grins, obsidian
eyes glint, and black hair, once thick
and lustrous, grows again, plays around
the porcelain.
                                        She is made to wear black
panties, black bra, black gloves, black
stockings, black heels, and a black smirk
stretched over perpetual mourning.

All black except her pale skin.

In a cocked helmet, she plants eyeteeth
for the soldier, always drunk, who deepens,
trying to evade, his hell.

She wants to erupt but can't and begins to see
that all the phosphorus of the ovens
can't burn out her eyes' dark wells.

# Buchenwald

Her hands join hands of scream that tear out hair
to wreathe her neck with knowledge. The surgery
of those whose shirt she wears has sheared her.

Is it you, Anna, shirtfront a ravine,
pants around knees? Are you so soon a saint?
I'll lay my body, weeping, by your wrecked house,
as once I marvelled, pierced by your firm vows
never to believe in evil or ever recant.

From this ravaged wood pure flames will leap.

She grins, holds hands with the invisible dead,
beckons, salutes with both hands, wrists
like rubber, tries to shake hair from her fingers,
then smiles again, her womb a falcon's nest,
an Aryan doctor's last ingenious experiment.

# The Dance

Whirling          entranced          the sergeant
          biting          her breast          she laughs

blood streams from his nails in her waist.
There's no pain like hers.
                              Not this.  Not this.

She polkas him toward his teeth on her collarbone,
the dancing blood.  Because.
                    She pivots, laughs.

And her rosy legs and buttocks have grown luxurious,
and strong enough to kill should the time come.

She whirls him with the fury of a conqueror,
toward his own off-balance oblivion, stuffing
her breast down his throat,                    not this not,
     debauching the rapist,
               she turns she twists she
makes rape war
          not this not this;
Her fingers alive on his skull
like wild serpents.

# The Nightmare: Ruth

She and the parents escaped, but she still whispers
to herself: Don't think.
                                        Karlsruhe was different
from the north, she said, the people lovelier, gentler.
She always smiles, her eyes vibrant and fervent.

Her two boyfriends were picked up by the state.

Now, with no shelter while incomings explode always,
she knows what those who stayed behind learned
about survival and daily freezing and burning.

From a ravenous cavity, the voices of rasping tongues
push her back, always, saying, Live! Tell!

She wakes with a worried smile, flushed and pale,
everything, all, as weightless as compressed air.

"There's a monster in my sleep doesn't want its name
known.  It's bad," she says, simply, smiling, "evil."

# The Assumption

Holy Mother, Madonna of the dark gown,
spun of human hair on the three-legged throne
of bone, you sit on cadaverous knees
while the three white doctors
of death continually bring
the bounty of your love flesh
from your child's limbs.
Teeth of the dead enclose your head like Magi.
Your sash is the pink of transparent bootees
which hang there.

In a stake fence of bones and piano keys,
a snaggled line, a lover opens
his abstract mouth of hunger
and tries to sing     while in that mouth
his killer lights candles to you,
the Whore of Auschwitz. Your hand,
severed, comes from elsewhere
holding his mark,
your lover's lowers candles,
his uppers flames.

# The Smile

*Picture the toilet as Dante's hell . . . .*

No, Hal, not this, not Dante's hell, this swirl
of dysentery and rain—no drainage, no change
of clothes; Dante never imagined such filth,
such evil, nor Chaucer's scummy Summoner,
in Satan's bung. Starvation stopped
menstruation, sexual urges ceased.
Bones in the skinbag holding her shivered.

It's a grip she can't break.
She smiles. Wrapped in a night of hunger,
a ravining victim plants teeth
in the fertile throat between her arm and breast.
She smiles, dark hairs leech,
ravens hatch, shriek.

Legs around her waist, hooves to buttocks,
how else is he whose ankles are hooves
to walk but with scissors,
how else whose sex is hunger to love
but with teeth? She smiles, engaged,
muffled screams searing.

## Ballet Slippers

She's a seated hearse, ravaged grave,
Whistler's mother turned toward the wall,
a child's saw-toothed mummy-box
on her head    blocking out the light.
Her eyes see nothing.

Death incarnate birth,
the end of maternity, cradling
a head-shorn, pink-stained girl
like a wooden doll on her shoulders;
footless ankles angle slightly upward.

She remembers, beside her, dancing,
nervously, flawlessly,
a small girl with long auburn hair.
The dance she's doing is only an exercise,
a form of magic that once had power
to please, a way of walking
toward death without falling.

That's all she does,
the only dance she knows.

## The Mask

Chewing the flower stems
of his ankles, a skin-clad lotus
collapses into himself
and lights on a spindle of hair
to become its hunchback.
Arms hang downward and meet
in an elbowed "V."

Barbarous thumbs
amuse themselves with one eye
of a small form their hands strangle.

Inside this spindle, the vacancy
of the human form is stretched
on a bitter puzzle it can't birth.

His head in a helmet of dreams
hangs from the stump of an arm.

Worms in the eyes of God's mask.

# The Locust Angel

Bald, bald, bald;
her breasts half-pink plums,

the pink slip under her shirtwaist
crumpled by a large hand
from an armature

Her legs dangle from a thumb

Cheek still flushed.
Grease for the fire.
Ashes. Exaggerations,
Pius says.
                    Small plums.

A cage of bones,
a locust shell, kneels
on the soldier's shoulders,
swallowing his head.
Its burly arms reach
down, to pull the girl,
tenderly, toward
a crude angel reaping
whole plantations

who finds these
small plums hard.

# Mother and Child

She hangs from a cross of blood
on a wall papered with the news.

> "KILL HIM," GERMANS
> YELL TO S.S. SOLDIER

(lower left column, page 11).
The people watched, it said.
(I am reminded of photographs
from the old New South.)
The killer's name was Kaduk.

The cross obscures the news:
Her ankles are fixed to the right arm,
the weight of her torso, a hammock,
levitated by nothing tangible, by threads
that tie a baby, belly to belly,
on her, both bloated by starvation.

Stock markets show general inflation.

Surely he's sleeping peacefully
and will wake into the care of the severed arm
pulling on these threads to keep them from falling.
Her legs shrink into the breasts
devouring her body to make milk.
He won't fall. They are too still.

Teeth grimace where lips have shrunken back.
Eye yolks burnt black exhaust the small print
of want ads recording, with names and numbers,
the details of desire.

# The Falcons

A leg has grown from the shadow
of a crossbeam
and locked her neck to the crossing.

Seven falcons
quilled with black hair
have torn a way to her womb
to build a nest.

This is only her nightmare.

Blood from her voice runs down
chin and front. Her last curses
or prayers trickle from her mouth.

As two hands stroke her throat,
her head falls back,
exhausted, appalled.

This cannot be happening.

Vitals entered,
the breath and heat
of a giant presence hovers
behind her. The god
who answers nightmares
has come to live here.

# #5602715

She hangs from a jagged fence.
The stakes of nations, jabbed
into her belly, lodge inside her chest,
pages from *Judges* pasted
over parts of her nakedness.

Buttocks and legs shrivel
to show in place
the door to the womb
whence Samuel issued
to instruct kings.

Remnant of Hannah,
maiden, wife, widow,

She strains to stand on her toes
in the air.
                Her hands reach down
in the frozen language of the eyes,
like a dancer's fingers
explaining abyss.

From this, Pius turned his eyes
to postulate a Jewish girl's
Immaculate Conception.

These arms and legs frail pillars.

# Prayerbell

Bones on his back ring a prayerbell,
he and the rider both wearing gas masks.

A small girl,
naked, with a fuzzy head, hangs

by her wrists. Her names are Esperanza,
Managua, Maya, Lima, Caritas, Inca,

Bolivia, Veridad, Colombia, Tierra.
Below his death-squad medals,

his left hand's a stained, empty
white glove.

Above them, his bloody-nailed
right rises in a "Heil!"

Bones on his back ringing a prayerbell.

# Owl

Head wide as shoulders,
eyes dark penniless pockets,
he lies awake, owl

of the waste places,
staring into his eyelids.
He's seen stubby facts

balms can never gloss,
eyes pulled toward brain's occlusions.

# The Hands

Birthright's labyrinth.

He's flesh and fragrance,
bloated and putrid green
in earth's gaseous ass.

No tunic nor cope,
no hair of illusion left,
the larvae unravel.

Hands without wrists hang
like fins.
                Even his cries
his own puffed throat muffles.

# The Pyramids

Though such starved eyes
seldom see outside themselves,
he sees dim future:

a naked mass (in
a small room where showers jet
gas) climbing itself;

the air shrinks without
scent, and the strong reach the top
to suck at brass jets.

The removed bodies
are burned, smeared with their own
vomit and excrement.

He sees mankind stripped,
packed in a rush-hour subway,
hurled through its own gut.

# The Pulse

White walls are covered
with the fine print of scripture,
gray as dirty snow.

They asked of those who
survived and escaped exile,
walls broken, gates burned.

Hands without arms, these
penguin flappers no longer
talk of edema.

This water-bladder
body inflates and deflates
with rotten breath of

the earth's commissars,
eager collaborators,
the Amazon red

with its lost tribes' blood.
Legs sticks below the knees, Chartres
built on bones like these.

Jerusalem's walls:
Old Gate, Dung Gate, Fish Gate, Gate
of the Guard, Fountain

Gate, Water Gate, Gate
of Furnaces, Tower of the
Hundred, the Broad Wall.

# Morning Prayer

I will lift up mine eyes—sheathed
in human bone.
        Whence cometh help?
        Distance cannot diminish
nor darkness hide
                this terrible paring.
This is the parchment of man.
      How goodly are thy tents.

       From this cut-out mouth
       all emptiness yawns.

Lord of worlds,
I will extol . . . my mouth speak
. . . beasts, all cattle, creeping things,

tokens of flesh and wings, torn,
                                        his kingdom
sealed in such small phylacteries,
of mute wailing, each with its small grains
of sacred dust.
                    No words, no voice,
to the world's end thou art
like grass that shoots up in the morning.

Man walks in a dream.  Depths cry out.

We can neither push off
nor pull down the miter of bone
we wear in the circling shadow.

# The Survivor

for Viktor Frankl and Martin Buber,
for the songs

You want me to make a speech?
Yes, I survived. Some of the best
did not. What's worse:
nightmares or their absence?
Sometimes I talk without stopping.
Specters conspire with my life,
threatening me with prophecies:
"Make meaning of sacrifice."
"Sacrifice? For what. Each found
something to suffice or nothing
to survive for. One man recited
songs he had made out of teeth.

There were two blooms on that bough,
and a woman who went up in smoke
looked out from this hut and said,
"I often talked to that tree."
"And does it reply," I asked.
"Yes, it says, 'I am here.
'I am life. Eternal life.'"
"Ah! Lebensraum," I laughed.

Since no man wanted to hear,
the Chinese poet played
to the gods on his jade flute,
then men inclined an ear.
So do these grim forms
long for men to clasp them,
for played on a flute of bone,
they aren't for the gods alone.

Then later he fell into silence.
There are silences heavier than stone.
None knows to whom they belong
or for or from whom they are kept.

# Leaf Song

In the factory of teeth,
ashes fall like snow.
Afterwards, snowflakes,
like little ashen people
cut out of membranes,
dance on soft winds.
But spring can't melt the ash
and the wind blows it away
only to bring it back in
a tangle of ribbons and hair
around a blank face painted
on a child's broken rattle.
These eyes are scissors,
these ashes seeds
the ground labors to absorb.
The white flag struggling
from the branch opens wilted
and slowly straightens its
creases. Sidewise, a small
body dances out. Hymen, O
Hymen, the scissors bleeding.
Look! Its veins are skeletons,
and every leaf's mouth
stitched shut.

# The Deputy: His Question

His poached eyes turn like haunted glass
from the shorn man at his side,
nail in the back of his neck sticking out
through his frozen tongue.

He knows the man's tied to earth and air
in marriage already consummate.

He's cut his own tongue out with silence,
Stolen his miter from the high priest of the Jews.
Their existence questions his authority.
His cope swarms with icons and pink handprints.

We did our best to save the converted;
many priests and Catholics were being killed;
we hoped a pact with evil might curb it and protect
our communicants and our international investments.
Consider, too, from our perspective, to rid Europe
of deviant views was not entirely undesirable.

These bloodless eyes make a choirboy of Caligula.
Who can look into those mirrors again
without seeing, behind their screen,
the mists of Auschwitz, Jesuit guidebooks,
and an S.S. convent grad        ordering
mothers queuing toward showers
to drop infants down chutes.

He stands by the cross, a fugitive
who knows himself,
and asks, "Lord, Lord, is it I?"

# Feeding the Multitudes

Back grown awkwardly to the beam,
he holds as his breastplate   a man
without eyes or lips   teeth
a closed zipper,   pubic hair
long like an old man's beard.

His law is paper.
He's cut a cross from Exodus
to pin to his miter.
His cope is pasted with its pages.

He has seen God in burning smokestacks.
His eyes wander in a wilderness:

Judgment, Death, Carrion, Nothing:
four falcons frame him and the cross,

a futile scarecrow,
                                        its tender hand a fist
arose in Egypt
                            and did not know Joseph
and fed the people guilt
and they ate it.

# The Peacemakers

White robes printed with faded icons
and one rectangular leaf of greened silver,
the old currency. Black robes
tied with a pink sash.
Shoes off: they stand on innocents
to raise celibate prayers, faces
scarred, visionary ovens
eating air and sun.

They had made peace with "Judgment,"

exorcised possessed virgins with red pokers,
broken the backs of angels with ingenious
doctrines, bartering women on the rack
of childbirth and motherhood, for fish,
featherless birds, reptiles,

but are fed and grieved amidst famine—
    eyes of charcoal,
    mouths of ash,
    hands of confusion.

*It sometimes seemed to me that his seizures of violence could come upon him all the more strongly because there were no human emotions in him to oppose them. He simply could not let anyone approach his inner being because that core was lifeless, empty.*

Albert Speer

You've all gone completely crazy.

Albert Speer's father

*I can prophesy here that, just as the knowledge that the earth moves around the sun led to a revolutionary alteration in the general world-picture, so the blood-and-race doctrine of the National Socialist Movement will bring about a revolutionary change in our knowledge and therewithal a radical reconstruction of the picture which human history gives us of the past and will also change the course of that history in the future.*

Adolf Hitler (1/31/1937)

*Our images of God, man, and the moral order have been permanently impaired.*

Richard Rubenstein

# The Dance of the Apes

*The borderline between man and the animal*
*is established by man himself....*
*We see before us the Aryan race*
*which is manifestly the bearer of all culture,*
*the true representative of humanity....*
*Take away the Nordic Germans*
*and nothing remains but the dance of apes....*
(2 April 1927)

*I am nothing but a magnet*
*which continually sweeps over the German nation*
*and draws the steel from the people.*
(24 February 1940)

Adolf Hitler

*Once I have settled my other problems, I'll have my reckoning with the church. I'll have it reeling on the ropes.*

Adolph Hitler (quoted by Albert Speer, *Inside the Third Reich*

*Ultimately the terminal expression of . . . rejection of reality must be deliberate self-destruction. The killer's final victim must necessarily be himself.*

Richard Rubenstein

# Hitler

"Bastard," they called me.
"Be a clerk," Papa said. Often,
he gave me hard blows for my good.
"Love-child," Mama said, "Leibkind,
whatever you do, it's you."
I tried several shapes, then played
a desperate people. My baton
was Nothung, Siegfried's sword,
forged in the loins that gendered
Luther. I played Wagner, he me;
moving through his arias,
I fed on the Volk-heart, it on mine.
Life against Law.
My needle stitched Il Papa's lips.
We understood the same Power—Me.
I cast an eye on his galleries
and tightened his barbed stitches.
He would have had to grunt out
my last rites had I repented
and not cut off my own thing.
We told him I was the Nordic Christ.
I freed the gold from the dark mouth,
woke the blond north and wed her
to the fertile south with a smoke-ring,
thus, filling my emptiness. "Goebbels,"
I said, "The gullet that swallowed
Borgias, Medicis and inquisitors
can stomach us." I made my pyre:
Europe, the Jews, Germany.

We tested the capsules on Blondi.
She didn't bark. With Eva,
my other bitch, I entered the cave,
the capital of the Thousand Year Reich
burning above us. My best work.
We bit the gelatin as I shot
myself. Now, the last rites:
"Here are my balls and blood.
Rip your stitches out,
Papa. Kneel. Eat, Papa—
with the new world.

# The Spiritually Confused

They swing in jungles, slither under swamps
and oceans. Elephants weep, whales shiver
as they move over us, under us, tapping virulence
within—wolfpelts lined with down of condors,
talons on glove tips, flippers from sharks:
Ape of the One over the many over the One.

Horses in valleys of buffalo fall;
great curvedhorns cackle in rain forests,
barren ewes howl on pampas. Scales tilt.
Hippos freeze in fjords; the giraffe's
neck, curt, chokes on the Red Danube.
Knives of glaciers open Chile and Peru.
A Bear tears Afganistan, an Eagle Nicaragua.

Pius swallows the gargoyle's tail, hangs
by his mute tongue from its bung; Chartres
trembles; nuns foal immaculately
through aryan eugenics; vampires nest in
their secrets; scorpions in wafers dipped
in vinegar sting the crucified. Freud cast out,
chimps ape scholars in Vienna's old halls:
wastes of comedic ideologies
dance in theatrical mirrors as apes of God
cornhole Luther, Eckhardt screaming, history
a bunker. Albino packs tear fawn from teat.

# The Alliance

This paperclip chain of command
twists the chain of being.
Scissors of dogma, shears
of history, wombs full
of paper, gunmetal
gray files, coffins.

This shelled brain
on the floor is God's
left eye, the shrunken
sun; these tangles,
his thousand scrawled names,
stick in our windpipes.

Categories crammed
into cattlecars, skin-draped
bonecages where incredible
birds shriek, still:
"Live to testify
and witness! Tell!"

# The Gibbons

Singing gibbons are more sensitive.
At daybreak each climbs to the top of the tree
he slept in, and every voice climbs
toward the sun, as their morning song rises
in unison. Beginning at the same E, pitched
in the same key, their scale rises gradually,
a half-step at a time, in cadence with the slow
crescendo of light rising from the forest,
each half-step always preceded by the E
they began with, until reaching the E above
their origin, their voices shiver
in a cadenza of ecstasy that settles
like a thousand fluttering birds into trees
rapt in silence. Then each gibbon slowly
descends and wholly goes about his day,
not stirred to virulence but cleansed.

Whatever they do to each other
or other primates, this unison with all
who celebrate each day the sun rising again
out of darkness bears no resemblance to those
mass rallies of blood and soil whose music gores
and fouls earth. Even we have this longing
buried within, to sing ourselves out of animal
origin toward new plateaus within, our voices
rising like moon-pulled tides to wash forests
with a song that descends but never falls
to those other unutterably backward depths
through whose unhealing wound legion bubbles.

# IN THE AFTERMATH

*If we are to study the nature of human evil,*
*it is doubtful how clearly we will be able to*
*separate them from us; it will most*
*likely be our own natures we are examining.*

M. Scott Peck, M.D.,
*The People of the Lie*

*The walls of a house that have been covered with the blood of martyrs must never be covered over or painted.*

*Excommunication must not be cast upon a city whose Lord has persecuted the Jews or constrained them to baptism, for the excommunication will remain in force even if the city changes its Lord.*

Richard Howard, tr., *The Book of the Pious*

# Crucidom

Mesdames, messeurs, Crucidom's fatal evince
of bigotry chasms deep wide and few wights
can cast at any and not delight mortality.
From most th'counts and no'counts of Yourup—
teachers, bankers, lawyers—up to the slattern
scrubbing the rotcellar floor—and in churches
like wildfire, two tumors tupped and hummmpt:
snow pure light, dark rancid sump—Adolf their
excessive sperm and spume, and a deadly error
it be to aware but Germ'ns, though, Just,
they themselves will, eons none can rent,
and many died and some lived good and just.
A ball twined: Stalin nodding night helped dead
crowns arise Hitler, Germany to shatter
with its yearning to hump like Francy England,
Druids, dissenters, Afrasians, or Jews for God.
Too, tatters of feudal loot bowed uncommon low
to die the Reds. Hitler was Yourup round a bend
down twisting curves, always mad for ranting
raids of plunder'n'pelf (or Jesus—What the Hell!)—
most times swizzling Jews to cost Crusades
on Arabs, as bellyvision left all blind'n'bent.
All naked, utterly blanched. Yourup, he thot,
waited him, like Upyour's Big Stick whut talked
soft but many reds skinned and slaves blacked.
There's no innocence desoured, no unvouring.
We be our own most fatal enema, M. & M.

# The Visitations

Burning out angers on oneself leaves more for those
close—any scapegoat or child—my mother's warps.
Her husband dead, she raised sons in the public
classrooms of her torn obedience to fathers
who nurtured a bullying South, pinching
my arm while smiling at others, when the memory
she praised in me, wanting help, helped what I
thought slips but learned were, to her,
the necessary lies of a widow's weeds.
                                        That voice
I tried to squeeze from my throat leapt out, back.
It's not her now but me.
                              Not all starve the child
in themselves or another, as we often did, wearing
benign faces. Lord, had we faces we want, not
the aberrations borne those we sorely love.

Mardi Gras gone, Lent on us, can these snow-capped
Alpes Maritimes cleanse glazed smiles or tears
from our Venetian masks, or recast the painted
newspapermash I shaped on clay for carnival?

Must I wear my ugly Pompeii, not scars of honor—
where are they?
                        Playing hero—or victim—can never
atone for the small deaths we live by, or try,
that scar us and others.
                                Camps where prisoners died
momently, do not make lesser forays on others
more bearable, the unlove we make, its daily wake.

Better never marry than be a prison where all within
either torture or burn.
                                And where do we learn?

# The Shape of Evil

I see Hitler as pattern of all injured rage—
never really human, *an unsexed zero at core,*
said Speer, his clone, yet we must find their
threads to follow them out of the maze, or be
swallowed by demonologies, abstract flat sticks
his victims became outwardly, *in extremis,*
as uniform skeletons.
Even our troubled mirror
joins us to him if blaming ourselves leads us
to blame others. Such voids want scapegoats,
and nothing fills them. Thirty million only
deepened his thirst. Thrown back on himself,
he wanted German blood. The eye of paradox,
all that saves us from ourselves or others,
never abstracts victims or killers, probes roots
to free us from strangling tendrils threading
bigots, blind to themselves, always. All cults
of Our Gang—purity, fitness, youth—shrink
and swallow truth.
How easily lies rule schools
or trades with deft or careless twists of fact
honed by the ridicule of kindred sycophants.

What crude instruments seed fertile fields
with rank unkillable weeds.
Desperate son
of a loathed father, he made corporal but not
art school, then cleverly sowed terror
to turn a fearful plantation into a Dwarfland,
psychically, physically, sexually screwed
with tics, obsessed with pornography,
the proprieties of marriage, tightly focussed,
glibly merciless in murder.

# Puritans

Puritans are rank pornographers. Consider
Victorians, or their children—Perfection,
Prostitution, Pedophilia, and Pornography,
those inseparable quadruplets—their erotica
for youth killed in light brigades or trenches—
blown up, machine-gunned, bayonetted, gassed—
for what frail reason or false peace?
Try to grasp total terror. People stripped
in streets, in their homes, in death camps,
Germany belly up under Hitler, half of Europe
bellying Germany—layers of pornography, death
camp on death camp, and some think it erotic,
people snatched—night or day—not to return,
all extraordinarily ordinary. Few opposed,
and many joined it by informing or by silence.
If some served to curb him, it was little.
And most, believing in their own high purity,
merely helped him soil Europe as he was soiled.

What ties us to threads hanging from the mouths
of Stalin, Vichy, and Christ's broker, with much
to lose, who ignored the crowing cocks of hell
for five thousand days of mass crucifixions?
Through five thousand massacres of innocents
he kept his pact with Hitler, dicing
for the remnants of Jerusalem. I was born,
bloody and screaming, into these lips of shame.

# The Moralist

There's the moralist in me. Anyone can play.
Who put coals of raving on my tongue, to sear
Pius, or the heirs of Kant, Goethe, Beethoven,
Bonhoeffer—three fingers pointing back.
We still keep peace with evil in our precincts.
Bigotry should taste sour for all time. Puke
fills our mouths while our nations make pyres.
We've seen Legion rise from lesions within.
Greed, obsession—God, money, race, more room—
some Manifest Destiny to kill or enslave:
Indians, Blacks, Hispanics, Jews. Germany,
like us, lusted for all, and while some face
this past, tasting ashes of ancestral ravaging
they repudiate from their depths, others deny it,
even as covens in cities of Bavaria rally
to old black, red, and white, in Los Angeles,
Greensboro. Business is good, high-tech thrives,
the land of total order still breeds aryan dreams,
its recent history shunted in schools, denied
at home, horrors houseled in the unconscious,
old bigotries proclaimed in the daily press.
We can't be cured until we name the disease.
Who lashes continents with bloody tails, struts
Chile, Afganistan, Iran, South Africa, Lebanon?
We sow history with fire and reap firestorms:
mustard rain, Hiroshimas of ash, Houston, Moscow,
building more systems for death than for life,
missiles mushrooming like steeples.

# The Cast from My Wife's Body

Istituto Ortopedico Toscana,
Firenze

Each afternoon they remove gesso. A cast
in the shape of my wife's foot and calf
lies on the overflowing barrel beside
a woman's empty arm, a hole for her thumb.
Gesso imprints of wrists, knees, torsos
litter the floor. The Tuscan girl
on the next bed is having the shape of her
left leg removed. Outside the room,
twenty or thirty gesso casts wait, bearing
delicate memories for burial or burning.
Each body part empties its eccentricities
into its plaster mold. Flesh under
the casts is yellow, green, purple.
No gangrene yet. Inside their legs,
their blood still carries away dead cells.

In Russia, Poland, Czechoslovakia, Hungary . . .
earth was dozed into gapes, like no body,
neither trench, ditch, canal, nor birdfish,
nor fleshflower. Nothing natural. If earth
opened them with quaking, all would be different.
Long lines of stripped women and children,
after a week's march forced into sudden
machine-gun fire knocking them into pits,
leaving behind their lugged belongings,
most of little worth to any but the dead,
but the soldiers had to work day and night,
for months to process these remnants of lives.
Under their own weight, these bodies, packed
like pressmeat in trenches airlessly sealed
from total rot, lost their shapes. Only
the soldiers, standing in rich air rising above
the bulldozed earth, looked, almost, like us.

# Surveying the Ravine

Have I locked myself too long in these poems,
as a friend said, a decade ago? Starving bodies
consumed themselves to live. I offer no puppets,
no masks of mirrors for our split selves,
our small engorging lies.
                                        We drift in rifts
where all injuries to civilization persist.
Outside in February, in thin-clad south France,
I read of America's new aid to old death brigades.
Ravine below, you back home, we don't get across.
I see the blue Med ten kilometers away by eye.
Beyond it, Africa, too, still tears in us.

Why are we split? Are my *white male gentile* pages,
one editor's words, made black by my breath?
I fight her clan's white sheets of babble—alone,
and against my own—as in trenches of childhood, still.
Is she greener, less bonded to, than I, our dirty
patriarchies of death, or cleaner? Am I more (or
less) monstrous by facing our face, if not whole—
or like my cousin—lymphoma bone cut from one arm—
who ever after had one arm and face of a child.

Do I ratify in these fires a father I never knew,
making all he is, loss my gain, unable to bond with
fathers I found too small. Dead fifty years, he stays
green, as he left me a good map long before my birth
when he ran away from home to go to school.

Can such poetry wash back home, or the politics
of our green beginnings still dream there?

# San Miniato al Monte

Above Florence

Still there, old countenance, milklight face
of polished marble articulate still
with dark green geometries?
And still unblemished by the syllabary
of agonies above which you watch
with your balance of silence? At dusk
you hold the sun until lights rise
out of earth to bathe you in brilliance.
You have seen tyrants and their stone walls
fall, rise, fall; Dante climbing
your winding knees, barred forever
from your vista of those magnificent
and treacherous towers; Brunelleschi's dome
swelling from Etruscan tiles
to cover the immense crossing's gaping
monuments to God no more than to the heart's
heroic heaving. And you witnessed the invaders'
grim machines of racial arrogance destroying
the subtle arches, the beautiful bridges,
where always *il popolo* go back and forth
the people, right and wrong, wrong and right
again—poets, craftsmen, engineers, merchants,
mothers, children—who swell with humanity
*in the mouth of the wolf,* cry, *Crepi il lupo!,*
kill him, then raise the bridges again.
Proud, alert, worldly, provincial, worried
because you watch over them, they accept
like you this constant traffic of pilgrims
back and forth over the quiet Arno
to revere shrines the heart has hewn
and houseled in time's magnificent hovels.
So faithless though we are, we climb again
the stations of the cross to steps that rise
from your knees like the beads of rosaries,
to look out on this city, above which, within
the terrible splendor of the suffering of men

(their crypts surrounding you, within you),
shimmering in Byzantine tiles and gold foil,
the ancient risen one, looking out
from the apse through the open door, weeps
His serene, silent, frozen light on the world.

# Rouault

He hangs from a gibbet
The red sun
wears a black ring.
Man is a wolf to man.

"I believe in suffering.
It is not feigned in me.
This is my only merit.
I was not made to be so terrible."

The society lady fancies she has a
reserved seat in heaven. Who does
not paint himself a face? We are
insane. We think ourselves kings.
Are we not all convicts?

The Chinese invented gunpowder,
they say, and made us a gift
of it. In all things tears.
War which all mothers hate. This
will be the last time, little father.

"I underwent then a moral crisis
I began to paint with an outrageous lyricism
It was an inner necessity."

For in turning toward his own inwardness
*he may become divided from things.*

The red sun always
wears a black ring.

# Chagall among Developers

He will spend his last days on a hill below,
near St.-Paul-de-Vence. Now, here, above Vence,
agents hound him for his view, his home,
where he works. On clear days, the Mediterranean
stretching one horizon and the Alps the other,
he inhabits the distances in this bright canvas.
Below, among galleries, villas, puzzled tourists,
posters emerge from the city walls at night
like stains stucco and earthen slips will never
really cover. These worry Algerians, citizens
as well as subjects, now, who often disappear.
Still, the agents dog him to their terms, build
tall villas around him, to wall him in and out.

He's the foreign one if they cannot imagine
his reeling brain needing this sky to house
gaunt forms he restored to laughing health,
many living only through him. If the agents
saw his Jerusalem glass abstractions—deep red
patches bleeding on a blue sky, orange sun
and yellow stars over an earth still green—
the language would certainly elude them.

But his bright oils prove how Provencal air
nurtures villages and fields from elsewhere.
Had one tried to explain how Chagall dissolves
time and gravity to give other realms in us
freer play, as he shows us everything, almost
clairvoyantly, like an impish Ariel swirling
pure pigments on a fluid surface, raising
necessary worlds where goats and cows graze
on flowers among clouds, naturally weightless
barns, synagogues, homes no longer there,
families and villages feasting at weddings
and mitzvahs, deliriously at ease, dancing
in this air again around rituals of innocence
from which they were spun, finally free, now,
of their heavy lives. You see?
They only shrug, *Realty is realty.*

***

*NAZI HORROR TOO TERRIBLE TO BELIEVE* **(headline)**
**by Ernest Cuneo—dateline Washington, about 1973 (excerpts):**

*Secret World War II documents published by the Vatican last week revealed that papal aides knew the Nazis were systematically killing millions of Jews.*

*Actually, ...there was scarcely an informed person who did not know ....*

*What is interesting and why it is still news, is that the mind of civilized man couldn't accept it. It was psychologically repelled as too horrible to be true.*

*For one thing, western man would have to revise his whole concept of the western civilization if it were. . . .*

*The justices of the court which tried and convicted the Nazi war criminals themselves had difficulty in believing the actual evidence. [Justice Biddle] afterward noted that there was extreme caution among his aides, one, a good honest fellow, particularly cautioning him that the witnesses had suffered much for many years and that their stories of atrocities, which indubitably happened, were nevertheless likely to be biased (A sensitive man, he repeatedly told Justice Biddle, "civilized people simply do not act this way.").*

*But when the actual pictures of the concentration camps were shown, with the piled up dead, and his mind could no longer flee the great truth, the man physically collapsed and had to be assisted from the courtroom.*

*The fact is the Nazis piled terror on horror by keeping hostages in reserve. As an example, when they marched into Vienna, the son of a Viennese professor made an impassioned speech against the invaders and was, of course, beaten and arrested on the spot.*

*His professor-father went immediately to a famous British journalist who stood in well with the Nazis and asked him to intercede, declaring that he was only a kid of 16 and he would take personal responsibility for him.*

*Within an hour the British journalist called him back and told him his son would be back the next morning. The next morning, the postman...accompanied by two Nazi guards...handed him a package.*

*The Nazi corporal said, in effect, "In the package are the ashes of your son. Call your British journalist friend and tell him your son is home. If you do not make the call, we will have another package for you tomorrow morning—your 18-year-old son will arrive home in the same way."*

*Of course, the Vatican knew of the Nazi atrocities, for among the victims were hundreds of thousands of Roman Catholics, some of whom accepted martyr's deaths at Auschwitz.*

# Aftershocks

*He who knows does not speak; he who speaks does not know.*
Lao-tse (tr. by Aldous Huxley)

*What if the absence of this involvement and the oblivion of this absence determined the entire modern age? What if the absence of Being involved man more and more exclusively to beings, leaving him forsaken and far from any involvement of Being in his nature, while the forsakenness itself remained veiled? What if this were the case and had been the case for a long time now? What if there were signs that this oblivion will become still more decisive in the future? . . . .*
*If the oblivion of Being which has been described here should be real, would there not be occasion enough for a thinker who recalls Being to experience a genuine horror?*

Martin Heidegger, "The Way Back into the Ground of Metaphysics"

*Vatican II's [1965] document, Nostra Aetate, or "In Our Time," was widely hailed as marking a major improvement in Catholic-Jewish relations. The statement specifically declared that the Jewish people should not be held responsible for the death of Jesus.*
*Throughout [1985], Jewish leaders have been meeting with church officials to discuss the meaning of the Vatican II document and what steps Catholics and Jews should take to promote dialogue . . . hoping that the church would go issue statements going beyond Nostra Aetate in opposing anti-Semitism.*
*"We are concerned as much about the actual composition of the text," said Rabbi Marc Tannenbaum, an official of the American Jewish Committee who was a signer of the international committee's [protest] statement. "The Pope's statement sang earlier this year with respect and affection, and that tone seems to have been lost in the technical gravities of this text. There's a kind of begrudging heavy-handedness about it."*
*The Vatican statement's only mention of the Holocaust was a sentence saying, "Catechesis should on the other hand help in understanding the meaning for Jews of the extermination during the years 1939-1945, and its consequences.*

Excerpts from an article in *The New York Times*, June 25, 1985

# Descents into the Dark Self, Ascents into Light

Aftershocks linger, few things in history are more documented, but some still look for its beginnings and endings, while others work hard to believe it never happened or is over.

The first question at early readings of these poems was almost always "Why did you write them?" The second was some form of "What's your background?" "Do you have a connection with the camps?" "Are you a violent person?" The questions invariably surprised me. What is there more important to write about? One publisher's reader—a decade ago—thought I should put the poems aside for ten years, in deference to survivors, and essentially I have done that, though several survivors had already read the manuscript and encouraged its publication. And a friend who recommended the manuscript strongly to her editor, was told that a "white gentile male" should not have written such poems. I am puzzled but not surprised by the complex censorship based on the accidents of my birth.

I could say that a catastrophe of such proportions (inflicted by people on people) makes victims of all. I could say that one wants to respond, as well as one can, in the medium one knows best, to etch the outlines of truth, and to make it vivid for others. These poems are about the viscous lake beneath the surface of our normal lives. They are not about normalcy. They descend into the dark self where dark selves merge, and knowledge of the dark may be the essential light. I make no claim for sufficiency. There can be none. Clearly these poems are disturbing. The facts disturb us, naturally, but beyond that, they tap into the Collective Unconscious—our dark sea of denial—of which the Holocaust was a manifestation.

The Nazi Party, in collaboration with Chancellor von Papen and the extreme right Catholic Central Party, came to power the year I was born. What *is* my relation to this? My father, a U.S. Navy medic who had served in the trenches with the Marines in World War I, died in rural South Georgia a month after Hitler's ascent, four months before my birth. When I was one and a half, my mother, a schoolteacher before marriage, left for a summer to renew her teaching credentials. I have clear memories of this period. I stayed with her parents, my teenaged uncles, and their small sisters. I remember screaming as my mother was leaving, my uncles teasing to ridicule my babyish fears, my mother laughing hysterically at their antics. Among other memories of early childhood, this one came back years later as a nightmare that fused with other fragments from a day I had never forgotten.

My uncles were not bad people. They all, for example, instilled reasonably high ideals in their children. I know that something like what they did to me was done to each of them, by older sisters, and by their parents, who altogether had ten children in a difficult time and place, all of whom finished high school, several of whom went to college. If they were above the norm in some ways, they were also quite normal in others.

When I was working on some of these poems—in the late eighties, I think—the news was full of a six-year-old child's long slow private hell and eventual death at the hands of foster parents—a criminal lawyer and an editor for a major publisher—both highly competitive and successful Manhattan professionals. Are we connected with this abnormality? Am I? If the answer is *No*, is it also *Yes*? I fear the qualities of character that nurture success while breeding division and perpetuating injustice in every sector of our society.

My father had to leave home to work his way through high school and then a year of college, before the trenches of France. He came back, taught a few years, then met and married my mother. Through work and ingenuity, he made a down payment on a farm and built, with used lumber, the house where I was born at the peak of the Depression. Before he died, he was planning to return to college.. He is a jig-saw puzzle of myth, like all fathers, and like the myth of America.

I enjoyed being thrown into the water and told to sink or swim when I was four. The water wasn't deep. All of my life I have loved swimming far out in lakes. Why was I not afraid? Another uncle, a school principal, exploded when, two years old, I touched his brown and white wingtips, newly polished for his date. He folded in my eyes like a shrivelled doll in a small casket. I have never liked wingtips, and I suspect those who wear them. My children have seen such cracks in me. What is under them? Where do they lead?

Where I was born bigotries were codified and conventional, and those who opposed them risked ugly or violent intimidation. My family would have opposed overt cruelty to blacks and favored "improvements" in the treatment of black people, but they did not question the system of segregration. They were normal. My poetry bleeds from such wounds, from an awareness that began at five when I noticed on Saturdays in our one-street, one-block town (where everyone stood in clusters as on a movie set) that blacks and whites were two separate cultures. And the blacks were warmer people.

My family wanted to help me, make me manly. My mother's laughter reinforced the system for doing so, and the severity of her punishment of my brother and me shocked even my uncles, though they treated their own children similarly. Her god was a patriarch, her brothers avatars.

These points, both cultural and personal, should illumine rather than trivialize our dualities. There are values in normalcy that society depends upon, ignoring any violence undergirding it. SS training required accepting humiliation from superiors and humiliating inferiors, rituals varying only slightly from those social and military rituals that many still feel bolster manhood and national security. When hazing in the military or in fraternities is periodically banned, after someone is maimed, scarred, or killed, why does it resurface and from where?

The best in our heritage is at best a thin veneer over feudal systems rooted in the id or the reptilian brain, far older than the ethos we euphemize as free enterprise and still send teenaged thousands to die and kill for on the other side of the world or next door, letting the bodies of the unfortunate here too fall where they may. Does not a system that rewards the most aggressive reflect the feudal past of overlords the SS saw itself heir to, only more purely and logically than we? We continually defeat efforts to create more humane systems at home or among small nations struggling under the feudal governments that enslave them, though it is clear freedom is the only hope the world has against war after war or more totalitarian solutions.

If I escaped most of the bigotries of my environment it was perhaps because my mother lived on ideals, as in a way my whole family did. One of their ideals was not to force their beliefs on others. Their church did not baptize children until they were old enough to choose. My mother believed in Jefferson's agrarian populism: those who live and work close to the earth have an innate goodness nurtured by that closeness. As a widow, a woman, and the principal and teacher in rural schools, she was treated by the crudest men with courtesy and respect. I knew their other side better than she. Though most were decent, some were quite split, and that split was (and is) widespread, close to the surface, violence ready to wage war or to become the mob of some dark orator willing to fan their fear, hate, and impotence and direct it toward the Other. The viscous lake has many jagged mouths, and there are always political and religious demogogues to give these mouths deceptive words.

Those who stand outside of normalcy see the gape and make others uneasy. It was clear to me from the first grade that I would never be an acceptable "Southerner" to those I was born among. In the third grade, like all American children, we were marched out like soldiers to salute the flag, say the pledge, and sing "God Bless America" and "Remember Pearl Harbor." We were all conscripted into a mass psychosis known as "the war effort." Cartoon posters of enemy leaders plastered the streets. These are the normal aberrations of any war, no matter how just or necessary. My initiations were reprehensible yet humane enough to innoculate, to preserve a vision of a province which wherever I go stretches into a world. Not so for many of the guardians of our culture, in almost all institutions, departments and media. I can imagine when and where and how they died the death they want to bequeath to us, spiritually and intellectually accommodated, like our schools, in our schools.

By the time I was weaned, the genocide in Europe had begun. Perhaps it had begun earlier: in the Hundred Years War, with the light brigades, Napoleon in Russia, at Verdun, in the trenches of France where my father was, where all the males from entire English towns were thrown into prophetic blankets of poison gas in order to defeat feudal powers that the Allies in turn replaced with fascists. It didn't begin in the 1920s with Hitler in prison, writing *Mein Kampf—my destiny, ours?*—for readers who were not made ill because they had been innoculated into a normalcy already prepared to compromise with bigots.

I was eight when the war first touched me, when one of my young uncles, even before Pearl Harbor, became a Marine to fight the Nazis and went to war tough and laughing. He lost his stomach to the jungle—where he still tries to work a radio in his *Guadalcanal Diary* photo. He spent much of his life between his bed and his wheelchair.

Until his death at 67, he ached with a tenderness he could never express except with the ironic barbs of the witty tongue he took to and brought back from the war and with which he spoke to everyone, including my grandmother, sharp as the bayonet he—half-hero, half-father—brought back from the war. I am glad he was not my father. He bullied his family and didn't like bullies. Always ready to defend anyone against injustice, even from his wheelchair. He worked for more liberal attitudes and practices in his church and his local Democratic Party. The last time I visited, he was on the telephone trying to help a black woman his age who grew up a mile from our house. He fumed about the red tape that frustrated efforts to obtain the benefits due her.

Her name was Mattie. I had not seen her since she was a young woman and I a child, though I had visited her brother recently. For several years they were our closest neighbors, and between us there was affection and respect. Mattie was never very warm to me, however, and even as a child I sensed that she felt sharply the injustice of racism. She and her brother had a quiet, aristocratic bearing very difficult for blacks to show then. He had one arm, and I liked talking with him as he went about his jobs with such relaxed competence and confidence, a whole, gentle man, secure in himself, protected by his absent limb. I remember going with my uncles to help winterize their house, a log cabin chinked with newspapers and clay, not very different from ours. This must have been a Christmas between my second and fourth birthdays, as my mother taught elsewhere before I was two and sold the farm when I was five.

Things did not get better. I was a lucky oddity. I had good friends every new place I lived. On rural schoolgrounds I knew the dark fringe, shadowy by day, that emerged at night. In college, I saw a director of religious education enraged at the thought of inviting a black person to play one of the wise men in the Christmas pageant. The kindly dean of students, father of a friend, wrote a searing letter about the idea of inviting black students with whom we had been meeting on their segregated campus to meet with us on ours. These things elicited from my uncle with the wing-tip shoes, principal of a high school, a racism more vile than I had ever seen in my family. In graduate school outside Chicago, I found the South I had wanted to escape. A black child in a children's home was refused by a "white" barbershop. Trying on a new shirt, he cried because he thought his skin was ugly. A genteel minister assured me he kept his congregation "homogenous." People tried to tell me racist jokes. Home, I found, was no place and every place in America. It was the age of hitchhiking, and I hitchhiked everywhere and freely. A Jewish friend was afraid to hitchhike with me. Everywhere I see what it's like to not have a white skin, but how can I imagine what it's like to be a visible minority in America, not to be able to "pass" in the danger zones without fear?

## Dealing with the Other

I remember violent arguments in my early teens with another uncle, who believed in segregation. He also believed in noblesse oblige, that feudal remnant of privilege by means of which the more fortunate are responsible for the less fortunate. It is a philosophy rooted in the doctrine of Divine Right, by which all things in nature are higher or lower forms, from God to the slug. The higher form has a divine right in the nature of things over those considered lower, and is obliged to rule kindly and benevolently. In opposition to the doctrine that all men are created equal, it stratifies the ranks of mankind into castes of more privileged and less privileged, noble and serf.

Regardless of any benevolent intent, positing Others as lower forms is a half-step toward their demonization, which is a half-step toward their destruction. In this dynamic, those of the higher rank are considered more natural, and we want to emulate them, reculturate ourselves to them. Those who deviate from our idea of what is cultured or natural must be corrected, punished, even killed. All religions and cultures seem to suffer such malaises, in the grip of which they transform Others into Satans or Devils, and devise means to purge them.

I thought of my uncle as an essentially good man who would not harm anyone. I was not frightened by the fervor with which he, and I no doubt, argued. So years later it surprised me when his daughter, who was perhaps eight at the time, told me how afraid she had been that he might hit me. Her reasons to fear his angers became greater as she became a more independent being. In the case of Germany (or Serbia or any group), in seeking cultural purity it became less itself, and not the Germany that German Jews had known.

To new generations, the Holocaust is vague, unreal, and Hitler is only a name for the cartoon demon by whom unreliable grandparents were revulsed. (In fact, those who seek to "purify" themselves or their cultures do become stick figures.) And there are others who never accepted or dealt with these events and want to push them out of memory or sanitize them, as they do the American past. Why remember these histories or dwell on the present imperfections of what may be the best nation on earth, affording more opportunity and freedom to more peoples of more races and religions than any other? The US is one of the earth's most pluralistic societies, though probably not the most just in its treatment of the Other. Yet as long as we fall short of our ideals, as long as one person is pinched by injustices that liberals and conservatives alike accept as in the nature of things, we must continue to work. To paraphrase Pelagius, *if we don't run, we go backwards*, for there are always those trying to revert to systems of privilege for themselves that are systems of death for others.

At no place am I arguing an equality between the Nazi system of genocide and other systems of injustice, here or elsewhere. Nothing in these poems should obscure the fact that the death camps, then and now, were unique, in their vast programmatic attempt to destroy Jews, to destroy Otherness throughout Europe—and not only during the period 1939-1945, as stated in a Vatican document issued June 24, 1985. The killing and the camps began early in 1933, when Pius XII made a pact with Hitler, and it lasted not six but twelve years. (And Hitler's antisemitic views had been published in vile detail a decade earlier.) When the Nazis entered Poland in 1937, hundreds of thousands of Poles were rounded up and killed in the first 24 hours. If a Polish Pope won't speak out unequivocably, what Pope ever will? *Yet this should not obscure the degree to which American systems of oppression of Others have also been programmatic, legal, and persistent.*

The rate of death during the war accelerated exponentially. The death machine, increasing in efficiency almost daily, funnelled trainloads to the camps from every point of Europe. No suffering compares with that of the Jewish people, who had nurtured a culture rich with intellectual, artistic, and social genius, despite centuries of repression. But the poor, the aged, the sick, and their children were the bulk of the victims, among the Jews also. Jewish loss and suffering was unique, will remain forever in the soul of every Jew, and should remain in the soul of every human. Numbers cannot measure the loss.

These poems deal with the effort of the mind to distort, deny, block out. Why are these poems as they are? Why not write about Vietnam—that tragic, often successful attempt by our government to deceive both itself and the American people. Long before My Lai, the American press uniformly refused to publish appalling photographs of "normal" Americans ravaging villages, laughter on their faces (shock? madness?), babies on their bayonets. I never wrote one of these poems without being conscious of the historic American impulse toward, acceptance of, or support for genocide and other forms of large-scale racial violence (against African Americans, Native Americans, the Vietnamese, Cambodians), nor the attempts of my culture to make me as a child conform my thought to the warped code around me. What is worth preserving in thought so frail that it intimidates children in order to preserve its self-deceiving image of America, of ourselves?

What terror afflicts those parents who do not want their children to know more than they know? What in the folk-heart wants to reproduce its own ignorance and narrowness? Why does a nation sworn to free enterprise sometimes inhibit a free market of ideas? Why, in a nation of prescribed universal literacy, do the schools teach less and less, causing many students to enter universities unable to understand what they read, barely able to express ideas intelligibly, afraid even to have ideas? And provosts are even now telling us that our universities must adopt corporate models, which means to cease to be universities. We speak of Basic Literacy and Functional Literacy but we fear real Literacy and increasingly avoid it. I have visited fourth-grade classrooms where there was one teacher for forty children. A third of the children could not read or write. Intelligent at play, they were zombies in class, and their teachers were worn down like packmules in Death Valley. They were black and white. That is in America. In Florence, I visited public schools where there were two alert and eager teachers for twenty interested and involved children of the same age. We are our own ghetto. And in the mid-90s, we are building more prisons than schools—as the proportion of teachers to students decreases and the proportion of administrators to faculty increases. That is the corporate model? What happened to the collegial model? What are we paying for and when and how will we pay?

Perhaps these poems began when our National Guard shot into a crowd of students at Kent State. That is, in fact, when I began writing them. Those shots silenced the protest of those who were being sent to kill or be killed, whose friends or brothers were dying in an insane war. They silenced the universities. How many children were silenced with that young man and woman who were on their way to class?

During the late sixties, passionate protest of our brutal policy toward southeast Asia—and our own sons—at times took fascist forms: antiwar protestors wearing Iron Crosses, destroying worksheets for a poetry workshop I taught on a day when a strike was scheduled against classes. Though glad to support the strike against an unjust war by meeting my class outside, I did not think one opposed stupidity by mimicking it, and the fact that the cause of the protestors was just did not make them less similar, when they confiscated and burned student work, to those students and professors who threw the books of the Other—Jews, socialists, and anyone the Nazis opposed—on the bonfires that Goebbels' rhetoric lit.

The Nazi weapons of death were only crudely efficient compared with means presently at the disposal of a number of nations. All we know about weapons is that once they are developed they can be used by crude leaders. All we know about our leaders is that, except for a few who rarely stay in power long, most show a crude understanding and inadequate humanity in the face of the human problems confronting us. There is no training ground for the kind of leaders we need. The people are not aware of the need. Our leaders come from among the ambitious, the compromisers, who accommodate power more than need. Leaders whose values and vision are commensurate to the problem do not reassure us with what we want to hear. We often prefer political leaders who threaten the ground of those who try to find common ground and roads to peace, and they leave them no road to self-respect except war or protest. This is a problem endemic to the civilization that condoned the first crimes of the Nazis, which in no way small led to conflagration.

I saw Mauricio Lasansky's powerful, life-size *NAZI DRAWINGS* at the University of Iowa Museum in 1970, as art students outside were floating "bodies" down the Iowa River to dramatize what we were doing to civilians and young Americans in Vietnam. (The news was full of My Lai, which the Pentagon called "the Pinkville incident"—a linquistic form of self-deception and denial, like that endemic in the Third Reich, which is a fundamental characteristic of all bureaucracy). When not on tour, the drawings are permanently housed in the University Museum. The "bodies" are on the bottom of the river, beached, or in the Mississippi or Gulf. Both sets of images persist in my mind.

At almost the same time I saw Lasansky's *NAZI DRAWINGS* (and a catalog of them with an introduction by Edwin Honig), I encountered *THE WARSAW GHETTO*, a book of graphically detailed drawings (seemingly representational) by Josef Kaliszan, made from memory after he had left Poland, with a text by Czeslaw Z. Banasiewicz. Lasansky's earth- and flesh-toned etchings evoke the Nazi atrocity in a vivid nonrepresentational symbology of the human form. So Lasansky and Kaliszan demonstrate the two possibilities available to any artist—the realistically drawn, though imaginatively shaped and selected, and the metaphorical. I use both approaches in these poems with the knowledge that some feel that metaphor cannot approach this subject. Both are always difficult and to varying degrees necessary to any writer. Shaw's dictum—all autobiography is fiction—leads us to its opposite in the nonfiction novel, which vivifies history rather than obscures it through its fictive frame. Facts can misrepresent, and the distortions of metaphor can reveal. We need better myths, not the absence of myth. Literal understanding might obscure facts more quickly than an imaginative one. The suppression of the imaginative by the literal, of humanisms by fundamentalisms, and of pluralisms by separatisms, are among the persistent malaises of the present.

Both *THE WARSAW GHETTO* drawings and *THE NAZI DRAWINGS* evoke the horror, in a symbolic drama that transforms but does not diminish the factual drama. In neither work is suffering shown with the same intensity as the reality behind it, nor can it be, but each artist gives us a fresh view of the suffering as he experienced it, both are artistically true, and both are powerful and disturbing.

Art inevitably distorts. The challenges for artists are to make the distortions illuminating rather than misleading and to avoid trivializing what must never be trivialized, even if necessarily inadequate. If the best art can do cannot be adequate, the attempt is no less imperative.

Many of the earliest of these poems began with Lasansky's drawings as springboards of imagery and expressive form, but the *Warsaw Ghetto* drawings also contributed imagery, and I was at the time examining other Holocaust documents, including photographs. I began to work on the poems seriously in 1971, after a year of further reading, when I had a summer research grant from Florida State University, and I continued to read, write, and revise over the next five years. Between 1976 and 1987, residencies at the MacDowell Colony, the Ossabaw Island Project, the Hambidge Center for the Creative Arts, the Karolyí Foundation in France, and the Virginia Center for the Creative Arts allowed me to pursue further difficult revision. I am grateful to these centers for the time and space to work.

All who have responded to these poems over the years have participated in the creative process, without being responsible for any of their shortcomings. I am indebted always to Larry Rubin and Donald Justice, friends as well as my earliest teachers, whose helpful early responses were generous and encouraging. Others whose response was generous and valuable include Philip Dacey, G. S. Sharat Chandra, Michael Mott, Hal Steven Shows, David Kirby and Kathleen Rugoff. Still others read one or another version of the poems and generously encouraged them. They include Judith Hemschemeyer, Alicia Ostriker, William Styron, Peter Cooley, Dr. Leon Wells (of the Holocaust Foundation and Library), and editors Paul Zimmer and Jonathan Galassi. Important criticisms and reservations have come from several readers, and I have considered their thoughts without always reaching their conclusions. I am indebted to former Florida State University professors Lawrence Cunningham (now at Notre Dame) and Richard Rubenstein (now president of the University of Bridgeport). The poems and I both have benefitted from the dialogue.

One anonymous reader called the poem "Hitler" "sadly, ludicrous." If Hitler did not literally castrate himself and offer the remnants of his body to Pius XII for communion, the world would have been better off had that black mass been performed instead of the one that was. The image of self-castration is Lasansky's, but the understanding of it is mine. Richard Rubenstein's analyses of the Nazi phenomenon are consistent with the view that the ultimate victim of the destroyer is himself. The SS was by any measure a perverse cult that combined ideals of purity with sadistic rituals inflicted systematically on millions, including pathological "medical" "experiments" on breasts and genitals. Some poems follow Lasansky's drawings in trying to express the perversion through sexual metaphor. Several valued readers felt that these images might appeal to voyeurism in readers, and though I have understand these concerns, it is difficult for me to see how in the present text this is possible. Sexuality and starvation are incompatible, and few of those imprisoned were biologically capable of sexuality. Moreover, Nazi law strictly proscribed intimacy with Jews. Still these extremes of dominance and intrusion were perversely sexual.

Rolf Hochhuth's play *The Deputy* was valuable also for his close research, which was published with it. Lasansky's images make the indictment eloquent and compassionate. In fact, the two Popes following Pius XII, cardinals at the time, were aware of the facts of the Holocaust and involved in the negotiations with the Nazis, but they never protested publicly. Anyone who has studied much Western literature and art has some Catholic education and a sense of the imminence and importance of the church. I feel for Pius XII as Hochhuth did and as Lasansky did. What I say to this man who claimed to represent Christ for the world, I say not in echo of Hochhuth or Lasansky but for all betrayed and for myself.

I read Richard Rubenstein's *After Auschwitz* when working on these earliest poems. His *The Cunning of History*, which should be read by everyone concerned with the problems of the present, was also of great value. The separate frames of the picture are so grim that we balk at the whole.

For a different, more personal and firsthand witness to the history of the rise of fascism and bolshevism in Europe, from its beginnings to the recent past, I am indebted to the published memoirs of Michel Karolyí, the first and last democratic president of Hungary, and of Catherine Andrassy Karolyí, both of whom were exiled from Hungary by Bolsheviks and later participated in the resistance to fascism during their exile, in both France and England, from the fall of the Austro-Hungarian Empire and the Triple Kingdom to the end of World War II. After the war, Karolyí returned to Hungary to become ambassador to France and Belgium, and the couple was exiled again during the Stalinist purges in the early 1950s. Both died in France. Their discussion of the roles of Western "democracies" in the rise of fascism can show us much about what we still do to ourselves and to less fortunate nations. Madame *Karolyí*, whose mind was clear and sharp during our several discussions a few months before her death in 1985 at the age of 94, was generous in her interest in these poems and in suggesting sources in her library, including her own discerning and informed writing.

Of other recent works that organized a personal research into the problem of the Holocaust, *The Survivor*, by the late Terrence des Pres, was extremely valuable. My poem "The Witness" is deeply indebted to that book.

Also, Kathleen Rugoff's Ph.D. dissertation at Florida State University, *The Holocaust in Recent American Poetry*, helped me avoid some of the more common images used in poetry of the Holocaust, but several of the poems preceded her thesis, and furthermore it is difficult to avoid entirely images that grow so much out of the reality.

An essay by Eli Pfefferkorn and David H. Hirsch is important for anyone interested in the patterns found in Holocaust literature. The essay is the afterword for one of the wisest and most triumphantly humane books by a survivor that I have read, *Auschwitz: True Tales from a Grotesque Land* (Chapel Hill: UNC Press, 1987) by Sara Nomberg-Przytyk, translated by Roslyn Hirsch. Every account by a survivor is necessarily a high act of courage and humanity, since it involves a reliving of the experience in memory. A very different but equally valuable book by Jean-Francois Steiner, *Treblinka*, was extremely important in clarifying the mechanism of the deathcamps as a demonic enactment of social engineering.

All works on the Holocaust witness to common phenomena, but in many voices and with different interpretations and conclusions about man and the human condition. They all show, however, that the reality experienced in the death camps (and throughout Nazi Europe, but far more intensely and absolutely in the camps) was an inversion of values we consider normal. In fact, the recognition of this fact seems to have been a requisite for survival. It is called an "inversion" of values. But in light of everything, is "aberration" a more precise term.

Nothing in these poems is intended to minimize, exaggerate or romanticize. The flat voice at the beginning of "The Survivor," offensive to one reader, is an echo of one of the voices found in Viktor Frankl's works, the distancing voice of a scientist that tries to report without sentiment, a voice that nevertheless can record the beauty of spirit in the woman he tells of, whose song I make of his telling.

In the later poems, the voices often take over. Some readers felt the strength of the earlier poems was in the objectivity of the speaker, but a few others worried that they did not know where I stood. It never occurred to me there was more than one place I could stand. I also felt that it was because of that objectivity that some readers asked for more relief and felt the poems, together—without more human voices to call us back from the abyss—too much. In the first poems, I did not feel free to enter the poem myself or see what business I had there, partly because I was trying to render Lasansky's drawings, to a degree, but also because I was an outsider. When I started developing an envelope of poems to surround the earlier poems, in France in 1985, I used a more personal voice. Later, with some reservations, I allowed the poems in the last part of the book to become more personal, and I spoke more as an American and as an individual. I am not there for myself, but for readers who wanted to know where I am and for those who survived whom I came to know.

In *The Savage God*, Alfred Alvarez mentions writers, like Plath, who became suicidal after immersion in the literature of the Holocaust. Whatever other reasons are involved for those writers, the initial experience is very depressing. No one can know what it is like to really be a survivor, and neither intellectually nor emotionally can we grasp it. But there was a point at which I comprehended a whole out of what I had heard the survivors say, and at that point they began to speak in their own voices, and I became a survivor at least of my reading and writing. They lifted me into light and out of depression.

I could not begin to cite all the sources that have consciously or otherwise entered these poems or this essay. When I began, I happened to be reading E.H. Gombrich's *Art and Illusion*, and it helped shape my view of the rationalizations in these characters and in ourselves. Gombrich was perhaps a more important influence on the poems than Lasansky, but he could have also been an important influence on Lasansky's paintings. Images and ideas found among psychologists and others have much to do with the pathology of these characters but little directly to do with poetry or the Holocaust. Studies of "alternate realities" are among these sources, not only for conceptions but for images. The source notes are those I recorded for myself as I read and wrote. Much was absorbed that was not recorded.

## Other Source Notes

***

*Like certain spiders, it puts its victims to sleep before killing them . . . . you put men to sleep, then you kill the sleepers. This may seem very complicated, but actually it was the only way.*

*

*The victor [of wars] is not the one who has lost the least men, but the one whose principle survives. The real stake of the war that the Nazis made on the Jews was life itself. When people talk about the war of 1939-45m tget confuse two wars that have absolutely nothing in common: a world war, the one Germany made on the world, and a universal war, the war of the Nazis against th Jews, the war of the principle of death against the principle of life.*

excerpts from Jean-Francois Steiner, *Treblinka*

***

*We cannot go on forever projecting Naziism and Stalinism as the examples of violence and negative values but must bring the question home to our own present world and ask whether science is itself a culture of negative values.*

*

[M]odern science has got itself into a position of being associated with the mechanical, with [rational intellect, and objectivity as] its sole value.

*

Some of our most 'modern,' 'scientific,' 'brilliant' minds seem to imagine that we can go on living as before, with the degradation and nothingness of the public experience expressed in terms of the historical myths and cliches that preceded it! But total death is not simply a myth-destroying reality. It disrupts more than those intellectual forms of mediation between man and his surroundings in religion, philosophy, scientific disciplines . . . . It tears apart . . . some of the forms of physical mediation. . . . Principal among these is the arms pile.

The notion that national 'defense' rests in the accumulation of suicidal weaponry is the final surrealism of the factual ethos, for total death is itself the mocking product of this delusion.

*

Fact is not superior to myth. Technology is not more efficient than religion. It was in th nineteenth century that the idea of men as gods came to us, and we still do not know what it means. The turbulence of our own century has produced advances in the idea of consciousness which we have hardly begun to absorb.

*Gil Eliot, The Twentieth Century Book of the Dead*
Allen Lane,The Penguin Press, London 1972 (pp.199-203)

***

The following are excerpts from a 1985 article in the
*International Herald Tribune*

Some of the most gripping testimony was provided by two Romanian Jewish dwarfs and sisters . . . who came from a circus family of seven dwarfs and three persons of normal height.

[She testified that] Dr. Mengele forced their entire family to sing naked [to entertain] Heinrich Himmler, the SS chief, and 2000 Nazi soldiers and officials . . . Himmler sat in the front row with a movie camera, enjoying the performance."

One witness . . . to spare him personal embarrassment[,] testified from behind a blanket . . . "[Mengele] gave me an injection in my spine. Half an hour later I was in a recuperation room [with other twins who had been operated on]."

The other men then told him that part of their sexual organs had been removed. An hour later, the anesthetic wore off and he was able to feel that a similar operation had been conducted on him.

Another survivor. . . recounted in an almost hypnotic monotone how she gave birth while under the authority of Dr. Mengele. Angered that he had not noticed her pregnancy beforehand, which would have prompted him to send her to the gas chambers, [once the baby was born] he forced her to cover her breasts with tape.

"He wanted to see how long a baby would live without food. The child got thinner and thinner, weaker and weaker. Every day Mengele would come and look at it."

A nurse in her bunkhouse stole some morphine and a syringe. . . . You want me to kill my own child," I said, I can't do it." We had a big argument until I did it. I murdered my own child.

"The next day Mengele came. He couldn't find my baby's corpse among the heap of bodies outside our bloc. He cursed me for cheating him."

***

From Peter Viereck's *Metapolitics:: The Roots of the Nazi Mind* , one of the first probing studies in America of the Nazi movement. his dissertation at Harvard) Knopf Capricorn Books, 1941, 1965:

*The most villainous church of all [to the Nazi ideologues] is the Catholic because it is the most international.* (p. 283)

*Dr. Engelke, a "German Christian," has said: "God has manifested himself not in Jesus Christ but in Adolf Hitler." An important pagan magazine, Der Brunnen: "How high Horst Wessel [the Nazi "martyr" killed by Nazi's as an excuse for beginning the rampage of terror that brought Hitler to power] towers over Jesus of Nazareth!" Hanns Kerrl is Minister for Church Affairs. In 1935 Hitler gave him dictatorial powers and the right to issue binding church edicts, including the power to dismiss or arrest clergymen at will. Kerrl in 1937: "A new authority has arisen as to what Christ and Christianity really are—Adolf Hitler.... As Christ in his twelve disciples raised a stock fortified to martyrdom, so in Germany today we are experiencing the same thing. . . Adolf Hitler is the true Holy Ghost." ... Hitler himself said: "We wish for no other God than Germany."* (289-90)

*In Hitler's concentration camps languish not only liberals and Jews but non-political and "Aryan" Catholic and Protestant miniser.... [The] courageous pastor Niemoller. . . is the most famous victim but only one of many thousands martyred for the crime of being sincere Christians. For example, seven hundred pastors were arrested in Prussia at one fell swoop in 1935 for denouncing modern paganism from the pulpit.* (p. 290)

*In 1936 the Evangelical Church Council, including Niemoller, sent directly to Hitler one of the most daring protests ever issued inside Germany. . . It quotes [Hitler's chief idealogue, Rosenberg's] demand that "the general ideas of the Roman and Protestant churches" must be trampled down as "negative Christianity" by the nations following nordic-racial principles." It expresses directly "to the Fuehrer our uneasiness that he is often revered in a form that is due to God alone." . . . The manifesto ends by posing "the clear question to the Fuehrer whether the attempt to de-Christianize the German people is to become the official government policy." ... Hitler's reply to this protest was still more persecution.* (p. 291)

# Acknowledgments

Fragments in the inset portion of "Buchenwald" were suggested by Galway Kinnell's translation of Yves Bonnefoy's *The Motion and Immobility of Douve*, and the italicized lines in "Mutant Aesthetics" were quoted--in a review by Catherine Andrassy [Karolyi] in *Horizon* IV/19 (July 1941) of Arthur Koestler's *Darkness at Noon*. Koestler's lines referred to Communism, rather than Facism, and remind me, at least, that the enemy we need to fear is not another so much as the enemy within.

Thanks are due to the following for permission to reprint poems they originally published, sometimes in variant version:

*Crazy Horse* for early forms of "Earth Goddess," "Buchenwald," "The Dance," "The Nightmare," "The Assumption," "The Smile," and "The Prayer and the Answer;"
*New England Review/Bread Loaf Quarterly,* Fall 1985, for "The Hindenberg;"
*The New Yorker,* for "Rouault," which is reprinted here with permission;
*North American Review,* for "Hitler" and "The Survivor;"
*Poets in the South* I/1, 1977, pp. 14-19, for "Earth Goddess," "Buchenwald," "The Mask," "Ballet Slippers," "Feeding the Multitude," and "Leaf Song;"
*Shenandoah* for "*Die Briefe*;"
*Southern Review* for "Edema," "Owl," "The Hands," "The Pulse;" and "The Hunger;"
*Swallow's Tale,* for "For The Nazi Drawings of Mauricio Lasansky;" and
*white mule* , for "Photo from the Eastern Front" and "The Locust Angel;"

"The Hindenberg," and "The Nightmare," were also included in the anthology, *Blood to Remember: American Poets on the Holocaust*, ed. by Charles Fishman. Indiana University Press. Versions of "The Behaviorist" and "The Faucets" appeared in *Articles of War*, Leon Stokesbury, ed., University of Arkansas Press, 1990. Versions of "Morning Prayer," "The Deputy: His Question," and "Feeding the Multitude"—were set to music, as *The Nazi Songs*, for soprano voice and eleven-piece wind and string ensemble, by William Averitt of the Shenandoah Conservatory, and first performed at the 1972 Yale Summer School of Music and Art in Norfolk, CT. These versions exist in private folio designed by the composer.

## About the Author

Van K. Brock has a BA from Emory University; and graduate degrees from the University of Iowa and the Writers' Workshops. Since 1970, he has taught at Florida State University, where he is a professor of English and a former director of the Writing Program.

Brock's poetry includes, *The Hard Essential Landscape* (Contemporary Poetry Series, University Presses of Florida) and several chapbooks, and poems in journals, including *The American Voice, Georgia Review, New England Review/Breadloaf Quarterly, New Yorker, North American Review, Ploughshares, Southern Review*, and *Yale Review*, and in anthologies including, *Strong Measures: Contemporary American Poetry in Traditional Forms, The Made Thing: Contemporary Southern Poetry, Blood to Remember: Poets on the Holocaust,* and *Sweet Nothings: The Poetry of Rock'n'Roll.*

Brock is the founder and former director of Anhinga Press, founder and former faculty sponsor of *Sun Dog: A Literary Arts Journal,* and founder and editor-in-chief of *International Quarterly*, a non-profit jounal of art and writing in all genres and from all origins.

# ANHINGA PRIZE FOR POETRY

| Selection: | Judge |
|---|---|
| **Ann Neelon**<br>**EASTER VIGIL** | **1995**<br>**Joy Harjo** |
| **Frank X. Gaspar**<br>**MASS FOR THE GRACE OF A HAPPY DEATH** | **1994**<br>**Joy Harjo** |
| **Janet Holmes**<br>**THE PHYSICIST AT THE MALL** | **1993**<br>**Joy Harjo** |
| **Earl S. Braggs**<br>**HAT DANCER BLUE** | **1992**<br>**Marvin Bell** |
| **Jean Monahan**<br>**HANDS** | **1991**<br>**DONALD HALL** |
| **Nick Bozanic**<br>**THE LONG DRIVE HOME** | **1989**<br>**Judith Hemschemeyer** |
| **Julianne Seeman**<br>**ENOUGH LIGHT TO SEE** | **1988**<br>**Charles Wright** |
| **Will Wells**<br>**CONVERSING WITH THE LIGHT** | **1987**<br>**Henry Taylor** |
| **Robert Levy**<br>**THE WHISTLE MAKER** | **1986**<br>**Robin Skelton** |
| **Judith Kitchen**<br>**PERENNIALS** | **1985**<br>**Hayden Carruth** |
| **Sherry Rind**<br>**THE HAWK IN THE BACKYARD** | **1984**<br>**Louis Simpson** |
| **Ricardo Pau-Llosa**<br>**SORTING METAPHORS** | **1983**<br>**William Stafford** |

# Other Books from Anhinga Press

| | |
|---|---|
| **Donna J. Long, Helen Pruitt Wallace, and Rick Campbell, eds.,** | **Isle of Flowers (An Anthology)**<br>**Florida's Individual Artsist Poetry Fellows** |
| **P.V. LeForge** | **The Secret Life of Moles** |
| **Gary Corseri** | **Random Descent** |
| **Michael Mott** | **Counting the Grasses** |
| **Yvonne Sapia** | **The Fertile Crescent** |
| **Rick Lott** | **Digging for Shark Teeth** |
| **Mary Jane Ryals and Donna Decker, eds.** | **North of Wakulla: An Anhinga Anthology** |
| **David Jordan and Hal Steven Shows,eds.** | **Cafe at St. Marks: The Apalachee Poets** |